COPYRIGHT

A WRITER'S GUIDE

To my stalwart
friend, Anne
Coker, a fellow
radical liberal
with love,

Michael Stivell

1-2-25-2020

Copyright: A Writer's Guide

By Michael S. Webb

Vision Press
4195 Waldort Drive
P.O. Box 1106
Northport, Alabama 35476

ISBN 978-1-885219-90-9

COPYRIGHT

A WRITER'S GUIDE

MICHAEL S. WEBB

Vision Press

The Author

Michael S. Webb, Esquire, is a Georgia attorney and published legal author. His law office is located in DeKalb County, Georgia, where he grew up after his family moved to Atlanta from his native State of Texas. He is admitted to practice before the Court of Appeals of Georgia, the Supreme Court of Georgia, the U.S. District Court for the Northern District of Georgia, the 11th Circuit U.S. Court of Appeals, the U.S. Tax Court, the U.S. Court of Claims, the U.S. Court of Appeals for the Federal Circuit, and the United States Supreme Court.

He has taught communication law and regulation as an adjunct professor at two Atlanta universities. He holds a B.A. Cum Laude in anthropology from the University of Georgia, J.D. and LL.M. (in Taxation) degrees from the Woodrow Wilson College of Law, and an LL.M. degree from Emory University Law School.

He is a member of the State Bar of Georgia, the Georgia Association of Criminal Defense Lawyers, the National Association for Public Defense, the American Bar Association, and the editorial boards of the *Georgia Bar Journal* and *Voice of Experience*, an ABA publication.

Dedication

This book is lovingly dedicated to the memory of my parents, Hon. Judge Charles Edwin Webb and Mrs. Mary Ella Webb, who made it possible for me to become a writer and a lawyer.

Acknowledgments

This is my first book, and I owe a debt of gratitude to many individuals for their support during its gestation and birth. University of Alabama Professor Emeritus David Sloan and his wife, Joanne, extended the offer to write this book five years ago for Vision Press. They gave me their blessings, despite the fact that I am a University of Georgia graduate and decidedly not a Crimson Tide fan, and they never faltered in their belief that I could deliver the manuscript (finally), even amidst a global pandemic.

My sister, Linda Kay Nash, and her awesome husband, Hollis, stood in for our late parents and gently nagged me to "write the damn book."

My Irish barrister buddy, Dr. Judy Jarecki-Black, who is a patent attorney, physician and doctor of philosophy in molecular and cellular biology and pathobiology, graciously read the manuscript and made suggestions. Thank you, Lawyer/Doctor Judy!

My three sons, Austin, Brandon and Christopher (known as the ABCs), cheered on their dad (as I knew they would do) from California and Florida.

A shout of thanks must go out in two different directions across the country to my accomplished author friends, Frazier Moore in New York and Steve Oney in Los Angeles. Mr. Moore, Mr. Oney and I belong to an exclusive club comprised of former editors of the *Impression Magazine*, our award-winning publication when we were penurious college students at the University of Georgia. Who let the Dawgs out? We did!

I am also grateful for the eagle-eyed proofreading services of my talented "international editor," Erica Brown, of Montreal, Quebec, Canada.

Last, my canine companion, Vesper, and my equine companion, Glory, provided inspiration for this dog and pony show. Of course, I bribed them liberally with treats — and to my good fortune, neither one of my furry friends has challenged my copyright to this book. In fact, they haven't said a word about it.

COPYRIGHT

A WRITER'S GUIDE

Table of Contents

Preface

I am a lawyer. Just an ordinary, solo practitioner. I am not an intellectual property (IP) lawyer. IP lawyers make gobs of money negotiating and litigating weighty issues concerning the literary rights of authors, composers, film makers and playwrights; the patents for inventions created by engineering and scientific geniuses; and the trademarks of giant corporations producing products we think are necessary for our survival.

Although my eager-to-learn journalism students at Georgia State University and Clark Atlanta University, where I taught communication law on an adjunct basis, addressed me as "Professor Webb," I am not Melville Nimmer by any stretch of the law or bloviated academic fiction.

In contrast, most of my days are spent lawyering indigent clients in jails and courtrooms who are facing serious felony charges. I battle prosecutors who seek to pirate away the liberty of my clients for the rest of their life. I suppose you could say that I am a street lawyer, rather than an expert on intellectual property.

So, what in the heck am I doing authoring a book about copyright law for writers?

My answer is the same as yours to the question you probably have asked yourself at times, i.e., what in the heck am I doing authoring a book or article on a subject beyond my ken?

We both do it because we have been gifted with the ability to communicate ideas to others through respect for, and the careful placement of, words. Of course, knowledge is power. Moreover, experience cannot be discounted when educating others.

If you revere the English language; if you read to better understand the world around you; if you slave over a keyboard, putting one word after another until you have a sentence, and one sentence after another until you have a paragraph, and one paragraph after another until you have a chapter and one chapter after another until you have a book; then you have the right to write about any subject you choose and feel good about your creation.

Fortunately, I am the son of a respected journalist who became a lawyer at mid-life, and then a judge, and after that a public information officer, speech writer and legal assistant to the chief justice of our state supreme court. My father taught me how to express myself in writing and speech, and he encouraged me to obtain a legal education which he said, authoritatively, is the best formal education in the world. He was right. I have never regretted studying the law or having the opportunity to write and teach others about the law.

I have taught the basics of intellectual property law to hundreds of college students majoring in communication as well as college students majoring in paralegal studies. I have worked as a journalist and a legal editor, and I have authored articles published in legal journals and chapters published in law books. I have worked as a piano player, singer, and songwriter in both bars and churches (but never in a house of ill repute).

Thus, I am comfortable, with writing this book as a guide for you as you write for the benefit of others. I have researched the areas of copyright law which I think are important to you, and I have endeavored to produce a book that gives you practical knowledge about copyright law you can apply to all writing projects you undertake.

This is not an everything-you-need-to-know-about-copyright-law book. I am cognizant that there is a lot to know about this subject that I do not know. Furthermore, I challenge legal academia and the copyright bar to name one lawyer who knows everything about copyright law in the United States.

Furthermore, this is not a copyright law book for "dummies." I find those titles insulting, and you as a writer should, too. You are intelligent and desire to increase your understanding about your duties, rights, and obligations as a writer. I wrote this book to complement your talents, not denigrate them.

Thank you for purchasing this book. While I must caution you that nothing on the following pages constitutes legal advice (you should consult a lawyer for answers to specific legal questions), I hope you will feel enlightened about copyright law after reading it.

Michael S. Webb, Esquire
Decatur, Georgia
December 2020

COPYRIGHT

A WRITER'S GUIDE

1

Introduction

Copyright Law from a Writer's Perspective

Ere we were two days old at sea, a pirate of very warlike appointment gave us chase. Finding ourselves too slow of sail, we put on a compelled valour; and in the grapple I boarded them: on the instant they got clear of our ship; so I alone became their prisoner. They have dealt with me like thieves of mercy, but they knew what they did; I am to do a good turn for them.

— William Shakespeare
Hamlet, Act 4, Scene 6

You are a writer, right?

This means you can spell.

You know when to use verbs, where to put adverbs, how to select adjectives, and why the placement of a noun can make or break a simple, declarative sentence.

You know not to dangle your participles or split your infinitives.

You know a gerund when you see one, even if you are unable to explain its place in a sentence to a friend at a cocktail party.

You have even diagrammed a sentence, once upon a time.

But you are not a lawyer, and you do not understand copyright law. (Heck, there are lawyers out there who do not understand copyright law.)

So, you need to read this book, for at least four important reasons.

Stated in Socratic fashion (i.e., as questions, rather than answers), they are as follows:

First, do you value your reputation for integrity and originality?

Second, do you want to publish more than one book or article?

Third, do you want to earn royalties for your journalistic or literary efforts?

Fourth, would you like to avoid being sued for plagiarism and copyright infringement?

If your answer to any of these questions is "no," stop reading now and enroll in a trade school. Study to become a master plumber or a licensed electrician. Upon graduation and certification, you will probably earn far more money in one week than you will in one year after you become a disgraced writer. And both of those occupations are honorable, worthy of respect, and satisfying, particularly when you go to the bank to deposit your earnings from plying your trade.

But if you wish to enjoy a long, prosperous career as a writer, whether you work for yourself as a freelance writer; pen magazine articles; become a nationally syndicated newspaper columnist; author nonfiction books; publish popular novels; write Nobel Prize winning poetry; make it big as a playwright; make tons of money as a Hollywood screen writer; or compose hit songs, then you must answer yes to all four questions. Otherwise, you will only be a legend in your own mind.

A successful writer must care about his or her craft. Sentences must be linked together to form paragraphs, which must be stretched into pages, which must ultimately morph into an original, intellectually honest manuscript.

To succeed as a writer, you must assemble a combination of vowels and consonants in a manner not previously done by another author. What you write for publication under your own name cannot be a product of outsourcing. Instead, it must be your own work product.

Let me state this another way. You cannot copyright a written work authored by another writer. Therefore, you need to have a working knowledge of basic copyright law.

Copyright law is all about protection — protection of the intellectual property that springs forth from your richly fertilized imagination. As a writer, you need the protection afforded your creative endeavors by copyright law. If we as a literate society wish to nurture and preserve the marketplace of ideas, then we must do so through copyright laws written for the protection of intellectual property.

I am both a lawyer and a writer, and I chose to write this book as a practical resource for other writers who seek guidance in matters of copyright law, but lack the time and money to consult a lawyer when a question arises about the originality of their work. A word of caution, however, is in order.

This book is not a substitute for legal advice, and the reader should always consult a competent attorney for advice and counsel on complex copyright issues. My late father, who was a wire service writer and news editor for more than two decades before becoming a lawyer (and later a judge), used to quote the cardinal rule of journalists: "When in doubt, leave it out."

But there are times when excising parts of a manuscript may

be undesirable, and an author may be able to avoid doing so by obtaining sound legal advice.

The purpose of copyright law is not to stifle the writer's creativity. Rather, the reason Congress enacted copyright laws was to foster and perpetuate original literary endeavors by protecting their creators from being victimized through piracy.

In the succeeding pages of this guide, my goal is to teach you how to protect the words you write for publication from theft by following basic rules of copyright law. This means you must also learn what the consequences are for ignoring basic copyright law.

Specifically, you will learn from this guide what can be protected under the Copyright Act, as amended by Congress, as well as what cannot be protected. You will learn what constitutes a valid claim for copyright infringement; the damages the holder of a copyright may recover in a copyright infringement lawsuit; and when a United States District Court judge may issue a preliminary and a permanent injunction against a publisher for a copyright violation.

The publishing industry, you most certainly know, does not operate in a laissez faire fashion, either in the United States or abroad. Publishing houses do not exist for the sole purpose of gratifying the egos of hungry writers. They are for-profit entities, and every word in every manuscript that they gather in — whether monosyllabic or polysyllabic — is assigned a specific dollar amount. Book publishing is not an altruistic affair. Competition among 21st Century booksellers is fierce.

The framers of the United States Constitution did not have the Internet in mind when they enshrined copyright protection for authors. Now, books can be purchased online and read using electronic devices. Online book sales, now conducted primarily by the giant bookseller, Amazon.com, have gerrymandered the marketplace of ideas into districts with harsh environments unconducive to the survival of the mom and pop corner bookstore.

Someday, what readers call a book may be known by another, foreign name from a novel written, perhaps, by Michael Crichton or Dan Brown.

This book, then, is all about writing the book as we know it now, by the book. This author's goal is to teach you to be careful in what you create (no Frankenstein monsters allowed), and to show you how to preserve and protect it. To eat? Or not to eat? That is the question for the writer, for whom this book is written.

2

Congress and the Copyright Clause

A Wee History Lesson

Cucullus non facit monachum.

It's one of my favorite Latin phrases. Literally translated (into English), it means, "The cowl does not make the monk." Most folks, including me, prefer to use it as the infamous proverb, "You can't judge a book by its cover."

But guess from which famous writer I stole this saying? None other than the Bard himself, William Shakespeare. Shakespeare employed this bit of wisdom in Act 5, Scene 1 of "Measure For Measure," and also in his play, "Twelfth Night," in Act 1, Scene 5 at page 3.

But wait a minute — did I say that I plagiarized this little bit of Latin from two famous plays written by Will Shakespeare? Or perhaps from Christopher Marlowe, who was Shakespeare's fellow Elizabethan of the same age, believed by literary conspiracy theorists to be the true author of Shakespeare's literary works?

If so, can I be sued for copyright infringement?

(I'll answer this in just a few pages.)

Yet, what if I really didn't steal it? What if I instead lied and said that I stole it, just to attract attention?

If true, then could my sentence stating I stole this from Shakespeare be introduced by the plaintiff as evidence against me at the trial of a copyright infringement lawsuit in United States District Court?

And if that is possible, would I be given the opportunity to introduce evidence to rebut the sentence that I wrote?

I'm hoping that you can see where I am going with this, but if not, let me just state for the record that the business of writing for a public audience can quickly become a sticky wicket. There's this pesky little law known as the U.S. Copyright Act of 1976. And there's another set of U.S. laws known as the Federal Rules of Evidence, which apply to the trial of a copyright infringement case and cannot be ignored. You see, the evidence admitted by the judge at a trial always determines the outcome of the plaintiff's case. Always.

Oh, what a tangled Webb I weave, you say. Oh, what a tangled web Congress has woven! If you don't believe me, just try to decipher and comprehend the series of federal statutes enacted by Congress to protect the intellectual property rights of authors, composers, inventors and map makers. (See Title 17 United States Code, Section 101, *et sequitur*.)

Yet, the real blame lies at the feet (the hands, actually) of the framers of the United States Constitution, who were prescient enough to write into that document an article that laid the foundation for our copyright, patent and trademark laws.[1]

Article I, Section 8, Paragraph 8 of the Constitution of the

---

[1] To be fair, credit is also due to the original 13 colonies, all of which, save Delaware, enacted their own intellectual property legislation upon becoming states after America defeated England in the Revolutionary War.

United States grants to Congress the power "To promote the Progress of Science and useful Arts, by securing for limited Times to Authors and Inventors the exclusive Right to their respective Writings and Discoveries..."

Notice the capitalization of the words, "Science," "Arts," "Authors," "Inventories," "Writings," and "Discoveries?" It is highly unlikely those words were capitalized because the framers of the Constitution had a cavalier attitude toward the rules of grammar and usage. Rather, the founders of our democratic republic grasped the importance of intellectual property to a young nation. They believed it was of vital importance to protect the legal rights of scientists, authors, inventors and other creators of intellectual property (most of whom were geniuses, by the way).

"The Congress" didn't waste any time doing that, either. In 1790, approximately one year after the Constitution became the law of the land, Congress enacted the first federal copyright law of the United States of America, known as the Copyright Act of 1790, published at 1 Statutes At Large, page 124.[2] Ironically, a large portion of the text of the 1790 Copyright Act was lifted, shamelessly, from the 1709 British Statute of Anne. One supposes that our forefathers in the First Continental Congress had a big problem with the way the United Kingdom's laws had been procedurally imposed upon the American colonies and enforced by the Crown, but not so much of a problem with the content and substance of those laws of England.

Although the Copyright Act of 1790's stated purpose was the "encouragement of learning," its main purpose was to protect the authors of "any map, chart, book or books already printed within these United States." But its drafters were careful to make sure that the protection applied to citizens or residents of the United

---

[2] If you're having trouble falling asleep at night, be sure to try reading the entire text of this law, which contains a run-on sentence worthy of the writings of Marcel Proust.

States and their executors, administrators or assigns.

In fact, the Framers were so bent on protecting the rights of America's creative types that one hundred years elapsed before non-citizens of the United States and material printed abroad were given any copyright protection, under the International Copyright Act of 1891.[3]

Like the Statute of Anne, the 1790 Copyright Act protected an author's original work initially for 14 years. However, unlike the Statute of Anne, the 1790 Copyright Act gave an author the option to renew his copyright for an additional 14 years, as long as he was still alive at the expiration of the initial 14-year term. To make the renewal stick, though, the author was required to record the title of the work during the six-month period before the initial publication of an announcement "in one or more of the newspapers printed in the United States, for the space of four weeks."

And of course, the author had to pay a fee to the clerk of the district court: a whopping sixty cents! The author could also get a copy under seal (essentially, a certified copy) of the copyright by paying the clerk of court an extra sixty cents for the copy. The author could request additional "certified copies" for sixty cents per copy. A bargain at today's prices, especially since the beleaguered clerk didn't have access to an early version of a Xerox photocopier!

By the way, you're probably wondering at this point exactly what the word "copyright" means. Below are excerpts from the definition of "copyright" from five different reference sources, three of which are dictionaries widely accepted by legal scholars:

Black's Law Dictionary: "The right of literary property as recognized and sanctioned by positive law. An intangible, incorporeal right granted by statute to the author or originator of certain lit-

---

[3] Charles Dickens was one of several unhappy popular foreign authors during this interval; he was denied payment of any royalties for his work in America, pilfered mercilessly by American publishers.

erary or artistic productions, whereby he is invested, for a specific period, with the sole and exclusive privilege of multiplying copies of the same and publishing and selling them."

Barron's Law Dictionary: "The protection of the works of artists and authors giving them the exclusive right to publish their works or determine who may so publish."

Nolo Press: "A bundle of exclusive rights granted to the author of a creative work such as a book, movie, song, painting, photograph, design, computer software, or architecture. These rights include the right to make copies, authorize others to make copies, make derivative works, sell and market the work, and perform the work."

Oxford English Dictionary: "The exclusive legal right, given to an originator or an assignee, to print, publish, perform, film, or record literary, artistic, or musical material, and to authorize others to do the same."

U.S. Copyright Office: "Copyright is a form of protection provided by the laws of the United States (title 17, U. S. Code) to the authors of "original works of authorship," including literary, dramatic, musical, artistic, and certain other intellectual works. This protection is available to both published and unpublished works."

If you think the definition in *Black's Law Dictionary* sounds archaic, you are spot on. It is archaic. The first edition of *Black's Law Dictionary*, compiled by an obscure, frustrated young lawyer named Henry Campbell Black, came out in 1891 and was published by West Publishing Company in St. Paul Minnesota. One hundred and twenty-five years later, boasting the 10th edition of Black's Law Dictionary, West remains a giant among legal publishers.

Why West Publishing Company's editors are still using Lawyer Black's original definition of the legal term, "copyright," one can only speculate. However, the *Black's Law Dictionary* definition does reflect the view of the Founders that a copyright should exist for the protection of literary property only. Yet, it is interesting that the Continental Congress also considered maps and charts as literary property, and treated musical compositions as books over the succeeding century.

Of course, the definition of "copyright" with which you as a writer should be concerned is that of the United States Copyright Office, which is organized under the umbrella of the Library of Congress. As you can see, the Copyright Office's definition of a copyright is much broader than the original concept contemplated by Henry Black, Esquire. The Copyright Office emphasizes that copyright protection only applies to "original works of authorship," although that protection is extended to original works, whether published or unpublished.

Of further interest is the fact that copyright protection, says the U.S. Copyright Office, includes protection for "literary, dramatic, musical, artistic, and certain other intellectual works."

What are "certain other intellectual works?" That's a good question, which I'll answer in a subsequent chapter. But let us return, for now, to our legal history lesson.

The Copyright Act of 1790 was not the last coach stop. Congress either amended or updated U.S. copyright law several more times: in 1831, 1861, 1863, 1870, 1909, 1976, 1988, 1992, 1994 and 1998. The 1870 change accomplished the transfer of federal copyright records to the Library of Congress. The 1998 revision is known as the Digital Millennium Copyright Act of 1998 (DMCA). It added criminal penalties to certain copyright infringement cases. These infringement cases are investigated by the FBI and prosecuted by the U.S. Department of Justice.

Some of the other changes in U.S. copyright law were made for the purpose of adopting international agreements in the form of conventions and treaties which established protection for U.S. copyright holders of literary and artistic works in foreign countries. These include the Berne Convention Implementation Act of 1988, and the ratification by the United States of the Universal Copyright Convention in 1954, and again in 1971. Most of the statutory amendments to the 1790 Act were made, however, to extend the longevity of the copyright term.

For your edification (and early warning system), your focus needs to be on the Copyright Act of 1976, which today is the meat of copyright protection at the dinner tables of American authors.

Prior to 1976, copyrights were protected under both state and federal laws. State laws cloaked unregistered works with common law copyright protection, while federal law gave statutory protection to registered works. The Copyright Act of 1976 abolished the dual state and federal copyright system, anointing the federal copyright system as king, whose reign began on January 1, 1978 and has been uninterrupted since then.

The Copyright Act of 1976 brought consistency to U.S. copyright law, which was a good thing, but the skiff did have a hole in its hull. If a writing or other work meets the subject matter requirements for a copyright, it must qualify for copyright protection under federal law; if it doesn't qualify under federal law, it is unprotected. No state law prophylactics are available for purchase by an author. The work must be original and "fixed in any tangible medium of expression," to qualify for protection.

The 1976 Copyright Act extended the term of a copyright to either 70 years or the life of the author, plus 50 years. Currently, thanks to the Copyright Term Extension Act of 1998, a copyright term can be either 95 or 120 years, or for the life of the author, plus 70 years. There is no longer any requirement for renewal of a copyright; the Copyright Renewal Act of 1992 removed that burden from the shoulders of authors who created their works on or after January 1, 1978.

If you are determined to not be ripped off as a writer (as you should be), what you need to know is this: Under 17 U.S.C. § 302(a), the duration of your copyright begins to run when you create the work by fixing it in a tangible form, and it lasts for the rest of your life, then another 70 years. However, if you are a joint author of a work, the copyright lasts 70 years past the last surviving author's death.

Some IP attorneys joke that the life of a copyright is dependent upon the existence of Mickey Mouse, who first appeared in *Steamboat Willie,* which was the first Mickey Mouse cartoon and the first animated short film by Walt Disney in 1928. This is because Disney and Mickey Mouse have been a driving force behind changes in copyright law since at least the 1976 Copyright Act.[4] For now, Disney's copyright of Mickey Mouse is scheduled to expire in 2023. To keep Mickey from being poached, Disney must persuade Congress, yet again, to extend the date of its copyright beyond 2023.

The Copyright Term Extension Act's 95-year fixed term generally applies to works made for hire (discussed later in this book). Briefly, a work made for hire is one which is created in-house for an employer. In that case, the employer is considered the author, and the 95-year copyright term runs from the year in which the work is first published. It is possible, however, to secure a copyright term of 120 years from the year of creation (of your magnum opus, not the world). Yet, the term of the copyright is determined,

---

[4] For a brief discussion of the "Mickey Mouse Curve," see Steve Schlackman, "How Mickey Mouse Keeps Changing Copyright Law," in Artrepreneur (February 15, 2014), available at https://alj.artrepreneur.com/mickey-mouse-keeps-changing-copyright-law/#:~:text=Under%20the%201909%20Copyright%20scheme,renewal)%2C%20expiring%20in%20 1984.&text=The%20maximum%20term%20for %20already,Mickey%20protection%20out%20to%202003, (*last retrieved on October 12, 2020*).

under 17 U.S.C. 302(e), by which period expires first.

And there you have it: the first segment of your journey, distilled in a few subsections of a federal statute predicated upon a clause in the United States Constitution. But copyright law is anything but simple. The relationship between the writer's work and the projection it enjoys under copyright law is complicated, and it can be quite frustrating for the writer.

Samuel Johnson once remarked, "No man but a blockhead ever wrote, except for money." I would add to his comment, after "except for money," the phrase, "and with proper copyright protection."

Meanwhile, I bet you have been wondering about the answer to the question I raised at the beginning of this chapter concerning my potential liability for infringing upon Shakespeare's copyright.

Well, here is your answer: there is no liability.

Why?

Because Shakespeare's works are in the "public domain."

What does that mean?

Be patient, and Ye shall know, before the winds into our sails blow.

3

Works Entitled
to Copyright Protection

Could Robinson Crusoe Copyright Himself? Nope!

Exactly what kinds of works can be copyrighted? The list is longer than you might think. It includes:

- Literary works (which includes computer programs, and even compilations)
- Musical works, including any accompanying words (lyrics)
- Dramatic works, including any accompanying music (scores)
- Pantomimes and choreographic works
- Pictorial, graphic, and sculptural works (which includes architectural plans and maps)
- Motion pictures and other audiovisual works
- Sound recordings (Vinyl, cassette tapes, compact discs, MP3s, etc.)

• Architectural works (Plans, drawings)

Furthermore, the works specified on the list are given expansive, not narrow, definitions by the U.S. Copyright Office. As you can see, some works can be registered in different categories. The thing to remember is that regardless of whatever category the work may be registered under, it must be fixed in a tangible form of expression. If a choreographer seeks to copyright a dance routine in a musical, the choreography must either be notated or videotaped. If a speaker wings it, the improvised speech must be written down or recorded to qualify for copyright protection. The same goes for performances: they, too, must either come from a written script or they must be recorded (using either audio, video or both) to be copyrightable.

What if you are the owner of a book, painting, manuscript or recording? Can you copyright your ownership? Nope. Although you've undoubtedly heard the old saying, "Possession is 9/10 of the law," in this case, possession gets you nowhere. Ownership of an object that is protected by copyright law, including the transfer of that ownership, does not give the owner or transferee any rights in the copyright given to the object. That's "no rights." Period.

How about if you are a minor — a child prodigy who has created a magnum opus or composed a symphony? Can you apply for a copyright, or does it have to be done by your parents or legal guardian(s)? Curiously, federal law does not prohibit a minor from obtaining a copyright. (Good news for budding Wolfgang Amadeus Mozarts!) However, a minor who holds a copyright has to bow to state law when it comes to assigning the copyright to another person; signing a contract with a publisher or performer; or making any deals, for that matter. Why? In each of the 50 states, minors are deemed legally incapable of entering into a contract during their minority. In legal terms, it's referred to as *capacity to contract* — minors just don't have that in the eyes of the law. The legal expression often used for this is *sui juris*, meaning (thanks to Lawyer Black) legally able to give consent: consent to marry; to make a will; to vote; to do adult things at last! In most states, the legal age of majority is 18 years, although in some states, certain adult activities, such as imbibing alcohol, are not permitted until one reaches the age of 21 years.[1]

What may be more important for you to know as a writer, though, is what is ineligible for copyright protection in the United States. Unfortunately, the list cannot be divided into categories defined by only a few words. The categories are broad, and they include, but are not limited to, the following:

- Any works that have not been fixed in a tangible form of expression (see the references above to choreography and impromptu or ad lib speeches and performances).
- Titles, slogans and short phrases; symbols or designs that are familiar to us; variations in typography, coloring or lettering; and lists of ingredients or contents. (Query: Does this exclude recipes? Not necessarily.)
- Ideas! Procedures, methods, systems, concepts, principles, discoveries or devices. (Note, however, that descriptions, explanations and illustrations are indeed copyrightable.) And.......
- Works that consist merely of common knowledge or information and thus are not owned by anyone, *i.e.*, works that have no original author. These are, for example, standard calendars, height and weight charts, tape measures and rules, and lists or tables that are found in public documents and/or

---

[1] This is probably a good idea, since scientific studies have shown that the human brain does not fully mature until age 25. And some medical-scientific types maintain that the brain is not capable of functioning at full capacity until about age 30. But does anyone ever use 100 percent of their brain power? So far, there is no recorded case of that — not even Albert Einstein could levitate objects and read folks' minds.

other common sources.

• Government materials. (Sorry to disappoint, but if you per-
chance obtain the plans for the final withdrawal of all U.S.
troops from Afghanistan, because you overhear a drunk general in a bar discussing it with another general, you just cannot write that down and apply for a copyright.)

But what about an original work embodying work excerpted
from a previously copyrighted work? Can you, as the author of an
original, previously unpublished manuscript in which you excerpt
material previously copyrighted by another author, obtain a copyright for your manuscript? The answer to this question is, "It depends."

It depends upon whether you have obtained permission, usually called a "license" from the author of the copyrighted material,
to include their work in your work.

It depends upon how much of the copyrighted material you
intend to use.

It depends upon how you use the copyrighted material in your
own book, which raises the question of ...

(drum roll)

... The Fair Use Doctrine, discussed in Chapter 7.

4

Biographies and Works of Historical Fiction

Can You Copyright History?

You can steal someone's time, but can you copyright it?

Nope.

You can borrow from history, but can you copyright it?

Nyet.

But what about writing and publishing a book based upon historical events? Does historical fiction pose any special protection concerns for an author? And is an historical figure subject to copyright protection?

If there are any trapdoors awaiting an author of historical fiction, whether poetry, a short story, or a novel, I have not tumbled through one. History consists of events; events are real; taking literary license of an event does not require a license. Of course, an historian's book about a historical event in which the historian interprets and comments upon the event's significance is eminently copyrightable. But taking a character out of the history books and plopping them down in a fictional setting in a fictional plot is perfectly permissible. Fair use is not even a consideration.

Interestingly, a biography of the United States of America's first president, George Washington, serves as the foundation for the doctrine of fair use in U.S. copyright law. Ironically, it birthed a poorly reasoned 19th Century legal opinion that former University of Georgia Law School Dean and Pope Brock Professor of Law L. Ray Patterson suggested was a candidate for the award of "first place in the category of bad copyright decisions." [1]

In 1834, Jared Sparks published a 12-volume work, *The Writings of George Washington, being his correspondence, addresses, messages and other papers, official and private, selected and published from the original manuscripts, with a life of the author, notes and illustrations.* (If there is a longer biography title anywhere in the United States, I have not yet found it. But see the title in the next paragraph!)

In 1840, Rev. Charles Wentworth Upham, a Harvard historian, published a two-volume work titled *The Life of Washington In the Form of An Autobiography, the narrative being to a great extent conducted by himself, in extracts and selections from his own writings, with portraits and other engravings.* (These were wordy times, it seems.)

While Sparks' 12 volumes totaled 6,763 pages, Upham's biography was a mere 866 pages and 353 of them were copied verbatim from Sparks' set. Approximately 34 of the 353 pages were verbatim copies from Sparks' biography, while 319 of the 353 pages appeared for the first time in Upham's work. Sixty-four (64) of the 319 pages were official government documents; 255 pages were private papers of President Washington. These private papers, calculated Professor Patterson, constituted 3.8 percent of

---

[1] L. Ray Patterson, "*Folsom v. Marsh* and Its Legacy" (1998), Available at: https://digitalcommons.law.uga.edu/fac_artchop/351 (Retrieved October 14, 2020).

Sparks' work.[2] Sparks sued Upham for copyright infringement.

The case was heard and decided in 1841 (the year future SCOTUS Justice Oliver Wendell Holmes, Jr., the nephew of Upham, was born) by SCOTUS Justice Joseph Story. Justice Story was sitting in an appellate capacity as a Circuit Court judge for the District of Massachusetts, which was not an uncommon task for a SCOTUS justice at the time.

Justice Story affirmed a lower court judgment in Sparks' favor, holding that Upham's copying of numerous private letters of Washington verbatim was not a "fair and bona fide abridgment" of the work under English common law.[3] Instead, it was piracy, Story ruled.[4]

Story's awareness in 1840 that a copyright was only available to an author when the book was published clearly influenced his bad decision to find Upham was liable to Sparks for copyright infringement. But the legal arguments made by the defendants were correct, at least on three points: (1) Washington's papers were not literary in nature; (2) Washington's papers were public and not private; and (3) Washington intended for his papers to be used by the public. Upham made fair use of Washington's private papers. Sparks did not own the papers, they belonged to the United States.

The fact that the first recorded decision on fair use was wrongly decided is an anomaly in American law. But as Justice Holmes famously said, "The Life of the law has not been logic. It has been experience."

Historical fiction is obviously a different genre than biogra-

---

[2] Id., at 433.

[3] United States judges, hearing cases and controversies in the courts of a country not yet a century old, relied upon English common law decisions in arriving at their rulings. Today, English common law is still the bulwark of many principles of American Jurisprudence.

[4] See also David Kluft, "A Presidents Day Copyright Story: George Washington and the "First" Fair Use Case" (February 17, 2014), Available at https://www.trademarkandcopyrightlawblog.com/2014/02/a-presidents-day-copyright-story-george-washington-and-the-first-fair-use-case/ (Retrieved on October 14, 2020).

phy. In a historical novel, an author may alter history fictionally, or create fictional characters, without fear of infringement.

My beloved University of Georgia anthropology professor, Dr. Charles M. Hudson, Jr., who was a leading scholar on the history and culture of Southeastern Native Americans and the expedition of mid-16th Century Spanish explorer Hernando de Soto, began writing historical fiction in the last years of his life. Dr. Hudson's historical novel, *The Cow-Hunter,* published posthumously in 2014 by the University of South Carolina Press,[5] vividly brought to life the birth of free-range cattle herding, which took place in the rich pluralistic culture and primeval landscape of colonial South Carolina.[6] Dr. Hudson's work did not infringe upon the work of another historian and became his sole intellectual property when he created it.

Aside from being insulated against copyright infringement claims, historical fiction offers the added advantage of shielding the author from defamation claims brought by estate of a bona fide historical figure used as a character in the novel. You cannot libel a dead public figure, for their reputation dies with them.

---

[5] Charlie Hudson (he will forever be Charlie to me), the Franklin Professor of Anthropology and History Emeritus at UGA, died in Frankfort, Kentucky, not far from the farm where he grew up, on June 8, 2013. He had been retired for 13 years. Charlie supervised my 1976 undergraduate honors thesis in Anthropology, which followed the lives of contemporary Creek Indians living in Macon, Georgia. He was a founder of the Southern Anthropological Society and he published several authoritative treatises, including *The Southeastern Indians* (University of Tennessee Press, 1976) and *Knights of Spain, Warriors of the Sun* (University of Georgia Press, 1998).

[6] Charles M. Hudson, *The Cow Hunter,* (University of South Carolina Press, 2014).

5

Copyright Ownership

Who May Claim a Copyright?

Copyright ownership is not restricted to the creator of a work. Copyrights can be owned by numerous different legal entities. This chapter 'splains it.

Animals

Perhaps the most intriguing copyright issue to emerge in recent years was, "Can an animal own a copyright?"

Indeed, a fierce 21st Century courtroom battle was fought over the issue of whether a human being is the only "person" who can own a copyright. The case made a monkey's uncle out of prominent animal rights advocates, as well as numerous seasoned copyright lawyers.

Although I like to refer to it as "The Case of the Grinnin' Simian," Dr. Greg Lisby, Chair of the Department of Communication at Georgia State University (who is also an attorney), calls it "The Case of the Smiling Simian 'Selfie'" in Chapter 13, "Intellectual Property," *Communication and the Law*, 2021 ed. (Communication Law Writers Group, Vision Press, Northport, Ala.).

But whatever title you give it, the case was most unusual, and some legal scholars denounced it as frivolous.

The central issue in the case was humorously framed by Dr. Lisby this way: "If a monkey takes a selfie in the forest, who owns the copyright?"

Not the monkey, ruled two federal courts. Although the monkey was silent about its courtroom loss, and Charles Darwin, likewise, did not comment, here is the interesting back story:

In 2011, a nature photographer, David Slater, traveled to the Tangkoko Reserve (a national forest preserve), in Indonesia, in search of a crested black macaque monkey that might be agreeable to posing for a wildlife photo shoot. He found one.

Slater and a group named Wildlife Personalities later included the photographs in a book published by Blurb. Slater claimed that a female crested black macaque stole the camera set up by Slater in the forest and took hundreds of pictures, including a self-portrait. The monkey denied this, however, alleging through counsel in a 2015 lawsuit filed on its behalf by PETA (People for the Ethical Treatment of Animals, Inc.) that Slater intentionally left his camera and accessories unattended so the monkey would find the camera and take some unique pictures.

Monkey see; monkey do, right? [1]

PETA alleged in its "next best friend" lawsuit against Slater and his book publisher that the monkey was a 6-year-old male, whom Indonesians researching forest wildlife had dubbed "Naruto." The gravamen of PETA's lawsuit on behalf of Naruto was that Slater and Blurb were infringing upon Naruto's [unregistered] copyright and thus ripping the monkey off. Naruto, not

---

[1] Vanity, thy name is not man, but simian!

Slater or Blurb, owned the copyright to the photos because Naruto was the photographer.

Meanwhile, the *Washington Post*, catching wind of the monkey shines, got into the act and published a story on August 6, 2014 about the wannabe Ansel Adams macaque (who was obviously not camera shy). The circus had come to town.

The case went to trial in the U.S. District Court for the Northern District of California (remember, federal

One of the "grinnin' simian selfies" in the legal dispute over who owns the copyright

courts have exclusive jurisdiction over copyright disputes), and Naruto lost. Although PETA alleged it was genuinely concerned for Naruto's best interests under the Copyright Act, PETA presented no evidence of a relationship with Naruto.[2] The U.S. District Court refused to grant a judgment to PETA "[d]eclaring Naruto to be the author and copyright owner of the Monkey Selfies with all attendant rights and privileges under law."

Yet, the fight over who owned the copyright to the simian selfie did not end until the U.S. Court of Appeals for the Ninth Circuit in 2018 upheld the district court's judgment, ruling that animals do not have legal standing to copyright photographs under the Copyright Act.

[2] For a thorough discussion of PETA's allegations and the responses of Slater and Blurb, see Matthew P. Hooker, "Naruto v. Slater," 10 Wake Forest L. Rev. Online 15 (http://wakeforestlawreview.com/wp-content/uploads/2020/02/10-Wake Forest-L-Rev-Online-15.pdf).

The appellate court did not rule, however, that Slater and his company held the copyright, which left the Monkey Selfies in the public domain. Apparently, none of the parties to the litigation anticipated this aspect of the Ninth Circuit's holding. Simply stated, the Naruto decision monkeyed around with copyright law.

The unusual ruling meant there was no authorship of the Monkey Selfies; nobody had a copyright interest in the photographs; and any human being (including David Slater) or business entity (including zoos) was free to exploit or use Naruto's works for profit. Animals cannot contract, bargain, or license creative works and thus cannot be recognized as authors.

Aside from raising ethical questions about the rights of animals, the Ninth Circuit U.S. Court of Appeals' majority opinion in the Naruto case is subject to an interpretation that Artificial Intelligence entities (AI) cannot "author" creative works. Although the United States Supreme Court has not spoken on this subject, it seems that nonhuman entities simply cannot author works that qualify for copyright protection. Human authors can exhale; it does not appear that writers will be replaced by robots anytime soon.

Corporations

In the eyes of the law, corporations are considered "persons" for numerous purposes. Thus, nonhuman "persons" can own the copyright to works created by others. Often, book authors will form corporate entities to hold and administer copyrights to their works. If you have ever read a David Baldacci novel, for instance, you will see the copyright symbol, the word "Copyright," the date and the words Columbus Rose, Ltd. on a page inside the book. (E.g. © Copyright 2018 by Columbus Rose, Ltd.)

A successful author earning large sums in royalties from sales of their works may have several reasons for forming a corporate entity to administer the copyrights to their publications. There may be income tax considerations. Channeling royalties through a nonhuman entity may reduce the effective tax rate on the author's earnings. Often, corporations, through loopholes in the Internal Revenue Code, pay less in taxes on revenue earned than individuals.

A different, yet equally important reason for having the copyright to a work held by a corporation may be protection of the author from liability in a copyright infringement action. If an author claims that their copyright has been infringed upon by another author, the correct defendant in an infringement action is the copyright owner.

If the owner is a corporation (and the corporation has been properly run), the author of the work may be shielded from personal liability if a judgment is rendered in favor of the aggrieved party. In most cases, the aggrieved author would be limited to recovering their damages from the corporation's assets (or insurance policy coverage limits), rather than the assets of the author. If the author who has infringed upon another author's copyright is held individually liable for the infringement (whether intentional or unintentional), it could spell the end of their financial existence and writing career, as well.

Other considerations could be the author's wish to remain anonymous as to certain works for personal reasons, or the desire for the copyright to a work to remain in existence, uninterrupted by the death or disability of the author. Unlike humans, a corporation exists in perpetuity, unless dissolved by a provision in the corporate charter; by a decision made by its shareholders and board of directors; by order of a judge in a lawsuit seeking involuntary dissolution of a corporations; or by the corporations division of a secretary of state for administrative reasons (i.e., the corporation has failed to pay its annual registration fee or file a required annual report listing its officers).

Estates

Corporations are not the only entities which can own the copyright to an author's work, however. After the death of an author, their estate may be the successor in interest to the author's copyright and continued earnings from royalty payments.

So how does an estate become the owner of a copyright of a deceased author?

Normally, this happens through a last will and testament made by the author which bequeaths intellectual property rights to the author's estate and gives a named executor the power to act as the estate's legal representative. The executor does not have to be a person, however; a bank or other financial institution can be selected as the executor of the author's last will and testament.

However, rather than giving the executor of the will, who is normally the personal representative of a testator's estate, specific powers regarding the author's literary estate, many authors choose to name a separate "literary executor" to administer copyrights and other intellectual property rights of their works. The literary executor is a fiduciary (a person who owes a duty of trust to beneficiaries of the estate) who is also charged with the duty to protect film, translation rights, the original manuscripts of the author's published works, and any unpublished or incomplete work (whether published posthumously or completed by another author).

The literary executor is also the curator of the author's "personal papers," consisting of correspondence, personal diaries, and records kept by the author about their works.[3]

Throughout the history of world literature, numerous famous authors named a literary executor in their last will and testament. These literary executors include Otto Nathan for scientist Albert

---

[3] Academia has a term for this "legacy of papers." It is the German word, *Nachlass*.

Einstein, Regine Olsen for philosopher Søren Kierkegaard, Paul Williams for novelist and playwright Philip K. Dick, Robert Baldwin Ross for Oscar Wilde, and Robert Hayward Barlow for H.P. Lovecraft. Franz Kafka, however, was reckless and died intestate (without a will). A good friend, Max Brod, dubbed himself literary executor of Kafka's works; yet, most of Kafka's literary estate was legally owned by Marianne Steiner and Vera Saudkova.

Sometimes, conflict may arise between the executor of an estate and the separate executor of the literary estate. This occurred with the Estate of Jan Michelle Kerouac, the daughter and literary heir of popular writer Jack Kerouac, when her own literary personal representative, Gerald Nicosia, clashed with her general personal representative, John Lash, in New Mexico over the right to make decisions regarding litigation in Florida in which Jan Kerouac was contesting her grandmother's will at the time of Jan Kerouac's death. The case was complex and resulted in a 1998 opinion issued by the Court of Appeals of New Mexico which affirmed the judgment of a New Mexico District Court that the general personal representative held the authority to represent Jan Kerouac's estate in the Florida will contest.[4]

Exhibit A is a reproduction of the paragraphs pertaining to the literary works of Jack Kerouac in Jan Michelle Kerouac's will which resulted in the clash between her general personal representative and her literary personal representative. Note that the clause in Section Seven of Ms. Kerouac's will enumerated specific duties and powers for her literary executor. However, the general executor named in the will was not granted explicit duties and powers in Section Eight of the will, which set the stage for litigation over who had the right to manage litigation in another jurisdiction.

---

[4] In Re: the Estate of Jan Michelle Kerouac, Court of Appeals of New Mexico Case No. 18,495 (decided September 11, 1998).

EXHIBIT A

"SEVENTH: I appoint JOHN LASH as General Executor of this Will for all purposes save those concerning any rights that I now possess or may hereafter possess in any literary works or literary archival materials, including but not limited to any literary works or literary materials of my father, JACK KEROUAC, and my own literary works and materials, including but not limited to Baby Driver and Train Song. As to these literary works and materials, I appoint GERALD NICOSIA as Literary Executor.

"In his capacity as Literary Executor, he shall make all decisions regarding the appropriate publication, republication, sale, license or any other exploitation of any nature of any intellectual property rights I have in any literary works or materials.

"He shall do these things with due regard to fostering economic return without devaluing or cheapening the literary works or any intellectual property rights flowing therefrom, or in any way reflecting negatively on me, my father, or my heirs or beneficiaries.

"In return for his services as Literary Executor, GERALD NICOSIA shall receive as compensation 10% (ten-percent) of any income generated by any publications, sales or other licensing arrangements that he has negotiated, payable to him at receipt of any such income by the estate.

"Such 10% shall be paid directly by the publisher, purchaser or licensee to the Literary Executor whenever possible.

"In the event of the predecease of JOHN LASH or in the event that he is unable for any reason or declines to act as General Executor as defined herein, then I nominate and appoint MAXINE BOWERS, my sister-in-law, as General Executrix of this Will, with the same power, rights, discretions, obligations and immunities.

"No bond shall be required of any Executor appointed in this Will; none of the Executors nominated in this Will shall be personally liable for any loss or damage in connection with the administration of my estate, except in the case of willful misconduct or gross negligence.

"EIGHTH: I authorize my General Executor to sell at either public or private sale, with or without notice, any non-literary property belonging to my estate and to invest any surplus monies subject only to any confirmation required by law."

6

The Public Domain

Exploiting Uncopyrighted Works: Don't Ask, Do Tell

What does it mean when creative materials are shelved under the label, "public domain?"

In its broadest sense, the term "public domain" refers to intellectual property that is unprotected by copyright, patent, or trademark laws. This intellectual property is owned by the public, not by the author, artist, or scientist who originally created or invented it. A work that is in the public domain can be used or exploited without having to obtain permission. However, no one can ever claim ownership of a work in the public domain.[1]

What's tricky about public domain material is that while an individual work belongs to the public, if someone assembles a collection of public domain works (say, in a book or on a website), the collection can be copyrighted even though the individual

---

[1] Except when the United States Supreme Court says it can be copyrighted, as it did in the case of *Golan v. Holder,* 565 U.S.302 (2012), discussed subsequently in this chapter.

works in the collection cannot be copyrighted. This is known as the "collective works copyright," and it is dependent upon the arrangers' creativity in arranging the works in the collection. An example might be a book of poems in the public domain grouped according to subject matter.

How does a work enter the public domain? There are four ways.

1. The copyright to the work has expired;
2. The copyright owner goofed in renewing the copyright;
3. The copyright owner "dedicates" (deliberately designates) the work to the public domain; and
4. The work is of a type that is unprotected by copyright law.

The Stanford University Libraries' home page has a link to a concise summary of each way a work may enter the public domain.[2]

A list of famous written works in the public domain is too long to publish here, but below are several titles, courtesy of Goodreads.com, that are shelved in the public domain, and their publication dates:

- The Picture of Dorian Gray, by Oscar Wilde (1890)
- Frankenstein: The 1818 Text, by Mary Shelley (1818)
- Dracula, by Bram Stoker (1897)
- Jane Eyre, by Charlotte Bronte (1847)
- Pride and Prejudice, by Jane Austen (1813)
- A Christmas Carol, by Charles Dickens (1843)
- The Time Machine, by H.G. Wells (1895)
- The Adventures of Huckleberry Finn, by Mark Twain (1884)
- The Adventures of Tom Sawyer, by Mark Twain (1875)

---

[2] Here is the link: https://fairuse.stanford.edu/overview/public-domain/welcome/ (last retrieved on October 13, 2020).

- Peter Pan, by J.M. Barrie (1911)
- Gulliver's Travels, by Jonathan Swift (1726)
- The Metamorphosis, by Franz Kafka (1915)
- Heart of Darkness, by Joseph Conrad (1899)
- Hamlet, by William Shakespeare (1603)
- The Adventures of Sherlock Holmes (Sherlock Holmes, #3), by Sir Arthur Conan Doyle (1892)

Can a work in the public domain be copyrighted at a subsequent date? Apparently so (at least in the United States) according to SCOTUS. In 2012, the United States Supreme Court ruled in *Golan v. Holder*, 565 U.S. 302 (2012), an opinion authored by the late Associate Justice Ruth Bader Ginsburg,[3] that Congress has the power to grant copyright protection to works in the public domain. The case was roundly criticized by legal scholars, with some even calling it "absurd," but one thing is certain: *Golan* upended nearly two centuries of the Fair Use Doctrine as it pertained public domain works.

Golan began as a lawsuit filed in a U.S. District Court in Colorado by orchestra conductors Lawrence Golan and Richard Kapp; musicians; and publishers, et al who previously had free access to foreign musical works in the public domain. However, Congress, tweaking the provisions of the 1886 Berne Convention for the Protection of Literary and Artistic Works, applied the term of copyright protection enjoyed by U.S. works to pre-existing works from other countries that were members of the Berne Convention.

Congress thus removed works that could be performed or recorded without payment of a licensing fee, such as Prokofiev's *Peter and the Wolf,* from the public domain, making them avail-

---

[3] Sadly, Justice Ginsburg died of pancreatic cancer on September 18, 2020, just before the beginning of the Supreme Court's October 2020 term. The legal world lost a brilliant American jurist and heroine of the movement for women's rights.

able for use only by permission of the copyright holder (not to be confused with Attorney General Eric Holder, the respondent in *Golan)* until the expiration of the copyright term for the work. This meant conductors and recording artists were suddenly subject to licensing fees charged by the copyright holder for old, familiar works in the public domain.

The legal issue in *Golan* was the constitutionality of Section 514 of the Uruguay Round Agreements Act of 1994, a law which implemented trade agreements with foreign countries seeking to equalize international copyright protection. Specifically, the Act granted U.S. copyright eligibility to foreign works previously in the public domain.

Lawyers representing Golan, Kapp, and the other plaintiffs in the original lawsuit had argued that restoring copyright status to works that had passed into the public domain violated the First Amendment because it interfered with the right to use, copy and otherwise exploit the works, and it interfered with free expression through these works. Because Section 514 of the Act violated the First Amendment, argued the lawyers, it also violated the Copyright Clause of the United States Constitution.

However, the Supreme Court rejected these arguments, holding that the Act does not violate the language in the Copyright Clause giving Congress the authority to limit the life of a copyright. Therefore, foreign works that were in the public domain prior to *Golan v. Holder* subsequently became copyrightable and subject to the Fair Use Doctrine.

7

The Fair Use Doctrine

All Is Not Fair in Law and Publishing

The Fair Use Doctrine of copyright law deserves more than one chapter devoted exclusively to that topic, but as all writers know space is king, and besides this guide is supposed to be concise. (Haha. A lawyer is supposed to be concise?) Still, for a writer attempting to determine whether appropriating parts of another writer's work for a benign purpose is a fair use, the doctrine is a nightmare.

The U.S. Court of Appeals for the Ninth Circuit in a 2012 opinion called the Doctrine of Fair Use "the most troublesome [doctrine] in the whole law of copyright," noting that legal commentators had criticized the legal factors used to determine fair use as "billowing white goo."[1]

So first things first: Like so many legal terms, "fair use" should not be interpreted literally; it should be interpreted legally.

---

[1] See *Monge v. Maya Magazines, Inc.,* 688 F.3d 1164, 1170-71 (9th Cir. 2012).

(*Cucullus non facit monachum*, remember?) What is "fair" about the use of another author's previously copyrighted work is oddly enough not defined in a federal statute by Congress (perhaps because Congress does not know what being "fair" means), leaving the definition of "fair use" subject to interpretation by federal judges (which could depend upon what they had for lunch).

This reminds me of President Ronald Reagan's speech on August 12, 1986, in which he famously stated, "The nine most terrifying words in the English language are: I'm from the Government, and I'm here to help." Writers have good reason to be cynical about the application of the Fair Use Doctrine — the United States government, acting through the judiciary, has not been particularly helpful to writers in establishing what is fair use and what is not fair use of copyrighted material. Yet, as the U.S. Court of Appeals for the Ninth Circuit pointed out in *VHT, Inc. v. Zillow Grp., Inc.*, 919 F.3d 723 (9th Cir. 2019), "Protection of copyrighted works is not absolute."

In other words, the defense of fair use permits a writer or publisher, in certain instances, to use copyrighted works owned by another without their consent. "Fair use both fosters innovation and encourages iteration on others' ideas, 'thus providing a necessary counterbalance to the copyright law's goal of protecting creators' work product,'" reads the Ninth Circuit's opinion in *VHT, Inc.*, quoting from its prior holding in *Perfect 10, Inc. v. Amazon.com, Inc.*, 508 F.3d 1146 (9th Cir. 2007) (a fair use case involving photos of nude models) and following the United States Supreme Court's precedent in *Campbell v. Acuff-Rose Music, Inc.*, 510 U.S. 569, 114 S. Ct. 1164, 127 L. Ed. 2d. 500 (1994).

Campbell was a seminal fair use case which sprang from a controversy arising when members of the rap group, 2 Live Crew, released a parody of Roy Orbison's hit song, "Oh, Pretty Woman," through 2 Live Crew's record company, Luke Skywalker Records. The song was titled "Pretty Woman" and was released despite

Acuff-Rose Music, Inc.'s refusal to grant the rappers a license to use Orbison's tune. But the Supreme Court, in an opinion authored by Justice Souter, held that 2 Live Crew's commercial parody could be a fair use within the meaning of § 107 of the Copyright Act.

SCOTUS, for the first time in *Campbell,* utilized "transformativeness," a concept not found in the Copyright Act, throwing a monkey wrench into the analysis of the first statutory factor for determining fair use. If a second author made a "transformative use" of the original author's copyrighted work, SCOTUS held, it is allowed as a fair use, to avoid stifling creativity.

Granted, under 17 U.S.C. § 107, it is considered fair (legally speaking) to use portions of a copyrighted work without permission of the original author or copyright owner. In other words, if you meet the requirements of this federal statute, you won't be subject to a federal court judgment against you for copyright infringement. But there are several requirements of the statute that must be met.

The threshold inquiry is whether the use of the previously copyrighted material consists of "criticism, comment, news reporting, teaching [which is interpreted broadly, to allow for the use of multiple copies in a classroom], scholarship, or research." If you can make a case for your use of the copyrighted material under one of these categories, then you move to the next batch of questions that must be answered in your favor.

Essentially, you or your lawyer (provided you exercise good judgment and consult an attorney) must pretend you are a federal judge (a scary thought), and consider four factors:

1. What is the character and purpose of the use? Is your use of the material commercial in nature (i.e., to earn bucks) or is it

for nonprofit educational purposes?[2]

2. What is the nature of the copyrighted work? Is it F. Scott Fitzgerald's *The Great Gatsby*, twice made into a movie and not exactly written with a charity in mind? (Hmm. Something to chew on here.) Or is it a passage from a concise tome about copyright law written especially for writers?

3. How much of the copyrighted material do you wish to use? And for those of you who are good at math, what is the proportion of the material in relation to the entire copyrighted work? And finally:

4. What sort of effect will your use of the material have upon the value of the previously copyrighted work? Will it impact the marketability or continued sales of the included copyrighted material by the other author?

These four issues must all be considered and resolved clearly in your favor before you climb out on the fair use limb. If you do this (preferably through a licensed lawyer who is competent in copyright law), your chances of being successfully sued for copyright infringement are lessened considerably.

Of course, the safest course of action is to leave the tree be and contact the owner of the copyrighted material or their literary agent for permission to use it. It is altogether possible that if what you propose to use and your purpose seems reasonable to the copyright owner, they might waive their customary licensing fee or agree to reduce your licensing fee to an affordable amount.

The question of what constitutes fair use of copyrighted material and what constitutes unfair use must be determined on a

---

[2] If the purpose for the use is commercial gain, the analysis is not likely to proceed past the first factor. See *American Geophysical Union v. Texaco, Inc.*, 60 F.3d 913 (2d. Cir. 1994), in which Texaco was nailed for allowing a company researcher to systematically copy scientific articles in a journal when Texaco had only a single use subscription and did not obtain the publisher's advance permission.

case by case basis in a United States District Court. This is because the Fair Use Doctrine, although codified in a federal statute, is essentially a defense to a copyright infringement lawsuit.

The latest SCOTUS (Supreme Court of the United States) case touching upon the Fair Use Doctrine as well as the concept of public domain was *Georgia v. Public.Resource.Org, Inc.*, 140 S. Ct. 1498 (2020). The case was narrowly decided, by a 5-4 vote. The Court's opinion, authored by Chief Justice John Roberts, was released on April 27, 2020. However, this time, Justice Ginsburg dissented, along with Justices Thomas and Breyer. Justice Alito voted with the minority but did not author a dissenting opinion or join in the other dissents.

Public.Resource.Org dealt a major blow to the legal publishing industry, but ironically, the public suffered collateral damage from the Court's decision. Public access to information was diluted, because legal publishers lost the financial incentive to publish state codes.

The controversy before the *Public.Resource.Org* Court involved annotations (summaries written by legal editors) of Georgia appellate court opinions interpreting the Official Code of Georgia Annotated (OCGA), a compilation of Georgia statutes by the Code Revision Commission (Commission) organized by legal subject and consisting of several volumes. The Commission contracted with legal publishing giant Mathew Bender & Co., Inc., a division of the LexisNexis Group, in a work-for-hire agreement to prepare annotations of decisions by the Supreme Court of Georgia and the Court of Appeals of Georgia (and in some cases, decisions by federal courts sitting in Georgia). A hard copy of OCGA in 2013 was sold for more than $1,000 to some purchasers, although Georgia residents could purchase a set of the OCGA volumes for just under $400.

The Commission contended that it held the copyright to the 186 volume OCGA, effectively having a financial stranglehold over

Georgia's citizens as well as Georgia lawyers. So when Carl Mala-mud purchased a hard copy of the annotated code and published the contents online under his Public.Resource.Org (PRO) website, the Commission was annoyed.

In 2015, the State of Georgia, acting through the Commission, sued PRO in the U.S. District Court for the Northern District of Georgia for copyright infringement. Rather humorous was the Commission's allegation that Malamud used a "strategy of terror-ism." Yet, the U.S. District Court ruled in favor of the State of Georgia, holding the annotations were eligible for copyright pro-tection because they were "not enacted into law" and thus lacked "the force of law." The District Court thus reasoned that PRO did not meet its defensive burden of proving fair use and issued a per-manent injunction which required PRO to cease distributing OCGA and to remove the digital copies of OCGA from the Inter-net. PRO appealed the ruling to the U.S. Court of Appeals for the Eleventh Circuit, which reversed the District Court.

The Eleventh Circuit reached back to 1888, relying upon the U.S. Supreme Court case of *Banks v. Manchester,* 128 U.S. 244 (1888) and applied the government edicts doctrine. In *Banks,* the Supreme Court held that "there can be no copyright in the opin-ions of the judges, or in the work done by them in their official ca-pacity as judges." (This reminds me of an old saying popular with trial lawyers. I have been unable to attribute it to a specific source, but it is this: "The law is in the judge's jaw.")

Historically, an edict was a decree or law issued by a king, queen, or other sovereign government figure. It was a form of pub-lic proclamation by the royalty of a monarchy. However, an edict is distinguishable from a public proclamation: an edict establishes the effective date of a statute, but a public proclamation is merely the declaration of a new law prior to its enactment.[3]

---

[3] The United States Copyright Office uses the technical term "edict of govern-ment" in a broad, comprehensive sense to include all written laws. The Copyright

SCOTUS agreed that the government edicts doctrine was dispositive of the issue in *Public.Resource.Org*. Reading between the lines of Chief Justice Roberts's opinion, it seems SCOTUS was not enamored of private legal publishers charging the public for a copy of laws enacted by their state legislature and interpretations of those laws by judges. The Official Code of Georgia Annotated belongs in the public domain, so held SCOTUS in *Georgia v. Public.Resource.Org, Inc.*[4]

The most celebrated (by some) case involving the application of the Fair Use Doctrine was *Basic Books, Inc. v. Kinko's Graphics Corporation,* 758 F. Supp. 1522 (S.D.N.Y. 1991) a U.S. District Court case. In a nutshell, the District Court ruled that a professor's course curriculum materials could not be copied, assembled, and sold by Kinko's Graphics Corporation as "coursepacks," without permission. It was not a use contemplated by Congress under the Fair Use Doctrine; instead, it was copyright infringement.

Basic Books, Inc. was an expensive legal lesson for Kinko's, which had paid roughly two million dollars ($2,000,000.00) to assorted publishers for the coursepacks without clearing it with the copyright owner. Corporate greed did not pay in this case.

You might surmise from the *Basic Books, Inc.* case that higher education is a business into which the Fair Use Doctrine likes to stick its nose, and you would be right. Universities are in the business of educating students to prepare them for a career, and education requires information access. Information is found in the libraries and computers of universities and, since much of it is therefore available electronically, disputes over fair use are bound to occur. One of them boiled over at an Atlanta, Georgia university with the largest student enrollment in the state: Georgia State University.

Office will not accept or process copyright registration submissions consisting of laws.

[4] *Georgia v. Public.Resource.Org, Inc.*, 140 S. Ct. 1498(2020).

Cambridge University Press v. Patton, 769 F.3d 1232 (11th Cir. 2014) was a case involving Georgia State University's (GSU) revised fair use policy, implemented in 2009 after GSU was sued by plaintiffs Cambridge University Press and other publishing houses for copyright infringement. GSU made a mistake in doing this while the lawsuit against it was pending, because it gave lawyers for Cambridge University Press ammunition to successfully argue in the District Court that the revised policy was inadequate and, in fact, resulted in continuing misuse of the fair use defense. GSU would have been better off in the litigation if it had not instituted its revised fair use policy, which required professors to affirm in a university form that the fair use policy permitted them to electronically post materials for access by students. GSU lost and the District Court judgment granted injunctive relief to the plaintiffs, thus prohibiting further electronic posting of the student materials.

GSU appealed to the Eleventh Circuit U.S. Court of Appeals, which nearly nitpicked the District Court judgment to death, opining that the District Court should have undertaken a "holistic analysis" rather than a mechanistic analysis of GSU's revised policy, which balanced carefully the four factors used to determine fair use.

Wait just a minute. A judge of a federal trial court should have used a "holistic analysis" in a case? Really? Anti-aircraft flak would have made been more useful in understanding the Eleventh Circuit's reasoning.

A year after *Cambridge University Press* came *Authors Guild v. Google, Inc.*, 804 F.3d 202 (2d. Cir. 2015), a landmark digital copying decision from the U.S. Court of Appeals for the Second Circuit, in which the boundaries of fair use were stretched beyond belief, in the opinions of copyright experts.

In 2003, Google, regarded as the world's most powerful Internet search engine, launched the Google Book Search Library

Partner project. In essence, Google transformed printed copyrighted books, through scanning and digitization, into an online searchable database. The transformation of these works for libraries was revolutionary, but a many authors and publishers were unhappy. Three authors represented by the Authors Guild filed a lawsuit in 2005, as did the Association of American Publishers, charging Google with copyright infringement.

The crux of the plaintiffs' arguments was that Google had not sought their advance permission to scan books that were under copyright before offering them to Google users. Google tried to remedy its mistake after the fact by crafting, with the litigants, the Google Book Search Settlement Agreement (GBSSA), which would have allowed Google to continue scanning the books if it (a) paid the copyright owners for the books already scanned; (b) agreed to a revenue program for future books to be scanned; and (c) permitted authors and publishers who didn't wish to participate to opt out of the settlement.

In 2011, however, settlement efforts were torpedoed by U.S. District Court Judge Chin, who was assigned to the case, over concerns about copyrights, antitrust laws, privacy, international law, and the potential release of Google from liability for future acts that might be illegal. The two lawsuits were consolidated for a joint trial. The plaintiffs moved to have the case certified as a class action, and Judge Chin granted class action status, but the Second Circuit, in an interlocutory appeal filed by Google vacated Judge Chin's order on the grounds that certification of the class was premature and remanded the case to the U.S. District Court. Upon the return of the case from the Second Circuit, Judge Chin rejected the plaintiffs' arguments that Google's actions were not fair use and granted summary judgment to Google, thus dismissing the plaintiff's lawsuit without giving them a trial.

It was the Authors Guild's turn to appeal, but the plaintiffs lost again when, on October 16, 2015, the Second Circuit affirmed the District Court's ruling, holding that Google's "project provides a public service without violating intellectual property law." The plaintiffs subsequently filed a petition for a writ of certiorari with SCOTUS, but SCOTUS declined to hear the case on April 18, 2016. That left the Second Circuit's judgment intact, giving Google the green light to continue digitize copyrighted works, using optical character recognition (OCR) software. In addition, other search engine companies were now free to digitize copyrighted works.

The U.S. Court of Appeals for the Ninth Circuit entertained an appeal in a similar, yet messier case, but the Ninth Circuit ruled differently from the Second Circuit in the Google case.

In *VHT, Inc. v. Zillow Grp., Inc.*, 919 F.3d 723 (9th Cir. 2019), the Ninth Circuit affirmed the district court's summary judgment in favor of Zillow, an online real estate marketplace popular with homeowners and prospective buyers to check valuations of property, holding that Zillow's use of 22, 109 copyrighted photos owned by VHT, the largest professional real estate photography studio in the U.S., constituted fair use. However, the Ninth Circuit's ruling seems contradictory (and confusing, at the very least), because that appellate court also affirmed the district court's grant of summary judgment to VHT, based upon a finding that Zillow had directly infringed upon the copyrights to 3,921 searchable photos owned by VHT. Zillow's defense of fair use regarding the latter photos didn't take, said the Ninth Circuit.[5]

Does the fair use doctrine apply to the use of photographic images in news reporting? This was the issue in the long-running legal battle between the Associated Press (A.P.) and a guerilla-style street artist named Shepard Fairey.

The A.P. claimed that a photograph taken by Mannie Garcia

---

[5] Somewhere in the mix was a U.S. District Court jury verdict in favor of Zillow based upon its fair use defense, but I must decline to translate the Ninth's Circuit's discussion about it into English. It is absolutely of no value to you as a writer, plus I don't have a headache remedy at hand powerful enough to justify telling you about it.)

for the A.P. of then Senator Barack Obama during an April 27, 2006 event at the National Press Club in Washington, D.C. was appropriated by Fairey without permission as the basis for the famous "Hope" campaign poster of President Obama. The A.P. accused Fairey of copyright infringement; Fairey countered by taking the offensive and suing the A.P. in 2009.

The stakes were high, and the legal issues were tricky for both parties in the litigation. Fairey contended he was encouraged by the Obama campaign to create the "Hope" poster but, in truth, the Obama campaign welcomed but never officially adopted the poster due to copyright concerns. Fairey claimed he did not profit from sales of the image; A.P. disputed this. Fairey maintained his use of the photograph was "transformative;" A.P. argued the opposite was true. Fairey and the A.P. were at a standoff.

The parties settled the case in January 2011 , however, with both sides refusing to surrender their view of the considerable case law interpreting fair use. Fairey agreed to not use another A.P. photo for commercial purposes without first obtaining a license from the A.P. The A.P. agreed to share the future rights to posters and merchandise bearing the "Hope" image with Fairey and to collaborate with him on a series of images he would create based upon A.P. photographs. Financial terms of the settlement were kept confidential.[6]

The "Fairey Tale" thus had a happy ending for both sides, and the doctrine fair use dodged a legal bullet. Surely, more shots will be fired at the doctrine by future litigants. The survival of fair use will ultimately depend upon the creativity of writers and publishers, the ingenuity of their lawyers, and the mindset of the judges determining the fate of their legal claims.

---

[6] Randy Kennedy, "Shepard Fairey and The A.P. Settle Legal Dispute," The New York Times (January 12, 2011); available at https://www.nytimes.com/2011/01/13/arts/design/13fairey.html (last retrieved on October 14, 2020).

8

Works Made for Hire

Giving It Up for a Steady Paycheck

Congress created another category of copyright ownership in Section 101 of the Copyright Act by providing for a "work made for hire." A work for hire is a work created by an employee under contract with their employer. Section 101 defines a work made for hire as

a work prepared by an employee within the scope of his or her employment; or a work specially ordered or commissioned for use as a contribution to a collective work, as a part of a motion picture or other audiovisual work, as a translation, as a supplementary work, as a compilation, as an instructional text, as a test, an answer material for a test, or as an atlas, if the parties expressly agree in a written instrument signed by them that the work shall be considered a work made for hire.

A work made for hire can be particularly advantageous for an employer; the employer merely pays the employee their salary while the employee is authoring the work. Absent an agreement in an employment contract to pay the employee royalties, the employer as the copyright owner retains all rights to profits (and losses) from sales, reproductions, licensing and adaptations of the work in stage, movie, or musical form.

Because Congress specifically provided for works made for hire in the Copyright Act, it is virtually impossible for the employee to allege and prove in court that the contract was adhesive or unconscionable because the employee lacked the power to bargain with their employer. Unless you are a highly paid in-house writer for your employer, you should be cautious about any employment arrangement in which you are creating a work for the benefit of your employer's wallet. Visions of literary or journalistic fame may be dangled in front of you, but don't be taken in. The royalty checks will be written to your employer, who will not be standing in front of the cashier line at the grocery store, eager to pay your tab.

Remember Dr. Johnson's wise advice, and don't be a blockhead.

9

Copyright Infringement

Those Pirates Stole My Magnum Opus!

Alas, both prosperous and poor writers may be either a plaintiff or a defendant in a copyright infringement lawsuit at some point during their literary career. In some instances, though, the writer's estate is confronted with a "hot mess" over a manuscript written while the author was *in esse*. (*In esse* is a legal term, in Latin. It translates into English as "in being" or "living.")

Writers do not live forever, but their words can and often do, enjoy eternal life.

Humorist Mark Twain, who wrote *Tom Sawyer, Huckleberry Finn, A Connecticut Yankee In King Arthur's Court,* and many other popular works, reportedly said, "I'm sorry to have my name mentioned among the great authors because they have the sad habit of dying off."

However, Twain did not realize how fortunate he was to "die off" and avoid becoming embroiled in literary litigation arising posthumously over an alleged copyright infringement. Such litigation has plagued the literary estates of some world-famous authors. The estate of the prominent Atlanta journalist turned novelist, Margaret "Peggy" Mitchell, is one of them.

Piracy or Parody?

Peggy Mitchell died at age 49 on August 16, 1949, five days after being struck by a car while crossing Atlanta's famed Peachtree Street with her husband, John R. Marsh. The couple was on their way to see a movie, "A Canterbury Tale." Eerily, Ms. Mitchell was struck by a motorist arrested for drunken driving and exceeding the speed limit at the intersection of Peachtree and 13th Street. Tomorrow would not be "another day" for the author.

Fortunately, Margaret Mitchell had the foresight to make a will before her death, and she left her two nephews, Eugene Mitchell, age 14, and Joseph Mitchell, a monetary bequest of $500 each. Husband John was named as the personal representative of Margaret's estate, a fiduciary duty that he held until his death in 1952. Stephens Mitchell, Esquire, who was Margaret's brother and an attorney, then became executor of her estate and fiercely protected the copyright to *Gone With The Wind,* guarding and controlling all literary rights, including the licensing of film rights and the sale of *Gone With The Wind* merchandise.

When Stephens Mitchell died, nephews Eugene and Joseph were the heirs of an estate valued at millions of dollars. Joseph Mitchell was well-qualified in one sense to look after his late aunt's literary works, earning an undergraduate degree in literature from the University of Georgia and a Master's Degree in English Literature from Georgetown University, in Washington, D.C.

But the cautious Stephens Mitchell had prudently created an *inter vivos* trust (a trust created during one's lifetime instead of by their last will and testament) for the benefit of Eugene and

Joseph. Attorney Mitchell designated Suntrust Bank as the trustee and transferred the copyright to *Gone With The Wind* into the trust.

Thus, when author Alice Randall penned and the Boston based Houghton Mifflin Co. sought to publish a parody of *Gone With The Wind,* titled *The Wind Done Gone,* in early 2001, it was Suntrust Bank that filed a copyright infringement action against Randall and Houghton Mifflin Co., in March 2001.

The Wind Done Gone, touted as a parody, was a novel about the life of the fickle Cynara (a play on the Japanese word for farewell, *sayonara*), the mixed-race, illegitimate daughter of a southern planter and his slave, Mammy. The satirical novel was written from Cynara's perspective and appropriated characters, plot twists, and various settings from Margaret Mitchell's epic *Gone With The Wind.* First, Cynara woos R.B. (Rhett Butler) away from her half-sister, Other (Scarlett O'Hara); then she subsequently dumps R.B. for a handsome, young, black male politician.[1]

Suntrust Bank succeeded through its copyright infringement lawsuit in halting distribution of *The Wind Done Gone* for a month and then obtained a preliminary injunction, in April 2001, which prevented publication of the book.

However, in May 2001, the U.S. Court of Appeals for the 11th Circuit, based in Atlanta, ruled the injunction was an unlawful prior restraint and permitted sale of the book.[2] The case was subsequently settled by counsel for Suntrust, Randall, and Houghton Mifflin Co.

The settlement allowed Houghton Mifflin Co. to continue dis-

---

[1] See "Murphy: The Wind Done Gone: Parody or Piracy? A Comment on Suntrust Bank, 19. Ga. St. U. L. Rev. 582 (2002-2003) and Michiko Kakutani, *CRITIC'S NOTEBOOK: Within Its Genre, A Takeoff on Tara Gropes for a Place,* N.Y. Times, May 5, 2001, § B, *available* at 2001 WL 2005875.

[2] See "'Wind Done Gone' copyright case settled," The Reporters Committee for Freedom of the Press, 2002; https://www.rfcp.org/browse-media-law-resources/news/%E2%80%98wind-done-gone%E2%80%99-copyright-case-settled.

tribution of the book under the label "unauthorized parody." Houghton Mifflin Co. also agreed to make a charitable contribution, at the request of Margaret Mitchell's estate, to Morehouse College, and adaptation rights were reserved by both the estate and "The Wind Done Gone" publisher regarding any future film and stage versions of the book, including sequels. Luckily for author Alice Randall, none of her rights regarding future adaptations were curtailed by the settlement.

Unintentional Infringement

Unlike parody, in which the satirists intentionally appropriate characters, scenes, and plot elements, an infringement may be unintentional if based upon a writer's subconscious memory of a particular portion of a work. Of course, whether an infringement is intentional or unintentional makes no difference under the Copyright Act, but an unintentional infringement may have mitigating consequences including an award of monetary damages.

Unintentional infringements occur more often, it seems, within the realm of musical artists. A singer-songwriter may be the victim of an "ear worm," hearing a melody over and over in his/her head without being able to recall its origin.

This happened to the late guitarist George Harrison, formerly a member of The Beatles, when he composed and recorded perhaps his best-known solo hit song, "My Sweet Lord," a paean to the Hindu god Krishna. Harrison's popular song received so much radio airplay that former Beatle John Lennon, known for his wisecracks, told a reporter, "Every time I put the radio on, it's 'Oh my Lord' — I'm beginning to think there must be a God."

Harrison's misfortune in being found liable for copyright infringement of "He's So Fine," composed by Ronald Mack and recorded by The Chiffons in 1963, stands out as the most well-known instance of plagiarism in American music history.

The case was styled as *Bright Tunes Music v. Harrisongs Music,* 420 F. Supp. 177 (S.D.N.Y. 1976). The trial took place in the U.S. District Court for the Southern District of New York. The court's opinion reflects sympathy for Harrison's unconscious use of the melody in "He's So Fine," for "My Sweet Lord." However, judgment was rendered against Harrison based largely upon an *appoggiatura* in "He's So Fine." U.S. District Court Judge Owen concluded (incorrectly, protested many musicians) the *appoggiatura* was a telltale "grace note" that was present in both recorded songs. Although the "grace note" was not in the sheet music Harrison ultimately released of the song, which he first recorded with keyboardist Billy Preston, the court relied in part upon the musical illiteracy of Harrison in finding that Harrison unconsciously copied the "He's So Fine" melody. Harrison had hired a musician with bona fide educational credentials to help craft the score of "My Sweet Lord," and this was a factor in the court's unfavorable judgment against Harrison.

At trial, an expert witness testified on Harrison's behalf to support Harrison's belief that the song consisted of how he sang it and not a composition captured in sheet music. Harrison's defense consisted, in part, of his stated inspiration from the 18th Century Christian Hymn, "O Happy Day."

But Bright Tunes Music also presented evidence from an expert, a pianist who played both songs for Judge Owen, and the pianist's rendering of both tunes was identical, as far as Judge Owen was concerned.

For what it's worth, I have shown my communication law students a video in which both songs appear side by side on the screen as the original recordings are played simultaneously. My students could not distinguish between the melody in the two tunes. While I do not know the extent of my communication law students' musical education, if any, I have extensive musical knowledge and performance experience in several different musical genres, including rock music (excuse my immodesty), and I too was unable to detect any appreciable difference between the melodies in each tune.

In my [humble] opinion, if law professors could somehow miraculously agree upon a textbook case for musical plagiarism, then it would surely be the 1976 case, *Bright Tunes Music v. Harrisongs Music.*

How to Prove Infringement;
Showing Ownership and Copying

All injury claims of a civil nature have a beginning date and an ending date for the purpose of asserting them in a court of law. This is known as a statute of limitations. It is when the legal clock starts ticking.

The statute of limitations for copyright infringement claims is three years. A lawsuit alleging that someone has infringed upon an author's copyright must be filed within three years after the date of the infringement. Judicial exceptions have been made to the three-year statute of limitations in rare cases only.

Infringement upon another's copyright, as I have discussed already, can occur in several different ways. Some of the more common types of infringements that wind up in court battles are:

1. An unauthorized, public display of copyrighted material;

2. The creation of an unauthorized derivative work;

3. Public performance of copyrighted music without obtaining a license;

4. Public use of recorded music under copyright that has been downloaded from the Internet without payment to the copyright owner; and

5. Creation of a new work which copies or borrows from a prior, copyrighted work.

Two basic elements must be proved to establish infringement upon a copyright: ownership and illegal copying. In theory, this sounds simple, but in practice, it is often a complex matter.

Proof of Ownership

Proving ownership of your copyrighted work comes first. If you cannot prove you are the owner of the copyrighted material, you will be tossed out of court on summary judgment without a trial.

One way ownership can be proved is by showing you have officially registered your copyright in the U.S. Copyright Office. Of course, to register the work means you must convince the Copyright Office that your work is of a type that qualifies for protection. This is not difficult, however, because works that qualify for protection are specified by the Copyright Act.

Registration, as I have already pointed out, establishes the date of creation of the work and ownership of the work. Although registration is not an essential of proof for establishing infringement, it is the highest and best evidence of ownership.

Furthermore, the evidentiary significance of registration cannot be diminished by the so-called "poor man's copyright." The latter is a myth that has been perpetuated for decade due either to ignorance or a misunderstanding of what constitutes legally sufficient evidence of ownership.

The poor man's copyright is a method in which a creator uses the United States Postal Service, a notary public or some other supposedly trustworthy official in an attempt to establish that they have legally possessed the intellectual property for a stated period of time. The poor man's copyright owner, in the event the intellectual property is usurped by another, claims that by this method they can prove a legally recognized date they first possessed the intellectual property.

This is farcical. U.S. copyright law makes no provision for

copyright protection using this method.

The poor man's copyright is not a substitute for registration. Section 101 of the Copyright Act of 1976, codified at 17 U.S.C. § 408, specifically provides that registration of a work is not a prerequisite to protection of a copyright. Furthermore, there is no appellate precedent in the United States recognizing the poor man's copyright as evidence of ownership.[3]

Proof of Copying

Proving someone has illegally copied a writer's protected manuscript is more difficult than proving ownership of the manuscript. Digital communication modes have blurred the definition of copying. Is it possible to appropriate or misuse a protected manuscript through an email, text message, facsimile, or a social media post? Of course. The difficulty lies in establishing exactly where in cyberspace the illegal copying occurred.

I have written a separate chapter, Chapter 14: Copyright in the Digital Age, that addresses copyright issues involving cyberspace, so allow me to give you the skinny here on the traditional way of proving that illegal copying has occurred.

In most cases, direct proof that an illegal work has been copied is unavailable to the copyright owner who has suffered an injury. Therefore, copying is usually proved through the introduction by the plaintiff copyright owner of circumstantial (indirect) evidence during a trial.

What is sufficient circumstantial evidence of an infringement? How can you prove a work was copied without an eyewitness?

First, you must present evidence that the "pirate" had access to your copyrighted work. This can be shown through the testi-

---

[3] See Eric Goldman, "How Will Courts Handle a 'Poor Man's Copyright?'" (October 26, 2016), http://blog.ericgoldman.org/archives/2016/10/how-will-courts-handle-a-poor-mans-copyright.htm (last retrieved October 14, 2020).

mony of a witness with personal knowledge of the access. Or it can be shown through admissions made by the pirate that they had access to the work.

Access can be established by proof that the defendant saw your work or had the opportunity to see or have contact with an earlier version of your work. Access can be established by evidence the defendant had knowledge of your work. If the defendant told another person they had knowledge of your work, testimony by that person may be admissible under numerous exceptions to the hearsay evidence rule. On the other hand, the evidence may not constitute hearsay and thus not be objectionable.

Yet, proof of access is only the first prong in proving copying. The plaintiff copyright owner must also prove that the work produced by the defendant and the original copyrighted work produced by the plaintiff are "substantially similar." The necessity for proving "substantial similarity" is premised on the policy of copyright law articulated by the Supreme court in *Feist Pubs., Inc. v. Rural Tel. Service Co., Inc.*, 499 U.S. 340, 361 (1991) that "not all copying ... is copyright infringement."

Suppose a journalism professor at a state-run university makes several photocopies of a news story in the *Washington Post* (WaPo), written by a Pulitzer Prize winning investigative reporter, for the purpose of teaching his students about the ethics of using anonymous sources (as Bob Woodward and Carl Bernstein did when reporting on the Watergate scandal). The professor gives each student a complete copy of the news story. The professor did not infringe upon the *Washington Post's* copyright of the story, because the copying was done for a nonprofit educational purpose. It was fair use. Copyright law encourages fair use of copyrighted material; such copying is not punished because to do so would be to stifle education.

But what if the journalism professor assigns his most promising journalism student to write an investigative news story for the campus newspaper and instructs the student to lift selected paragraphs from the WaPo story and use them verbatim in the student's news story, without attribution, and to lift other paragraphs for use, but alter them slightly? This copying is almost certainly infringement, because the student's news story and the WaPo news story are substantially similar.

Unfortunately, proof of substantial similarity is not always clear, as in the preceding example. Making a finding of fact regarding similarity may require a swim through murky waters. Exactly what is "substantial similarity?" Is there a bright line rule courts consistently apply or a litmus test universally used for determining whether a new work bears a substantial similarity to an older work? Not really.

The concept of "substantial similarity" calls for a subjective judgment by the trier of fact, which provides no uniformity in the law on a case by case basis. Lawyers, jurists, and legal scholars have struggled to define this complicated concept, and they have disagreed about the correct approach.

In 2014, a research study on determining substantial similarity was published in the *Iowa Law Review* by three law professors; two were on the faculty of the University of Pennsylvania Law School and the third was on the faculty of the Maurice A. Deane School of Law at Hofstra University. One of the Penn Law professors, Tess Wilkinson-Ryan, was an assistant professor of law and psychology.

(See Shyamkrishna Balganesh, Irina D. Manta, and Tess Wilkinson-Ryan, *Judging Similarity,* 100 Iowa L. Rev. (2014), abstract available at http://ssrn.com/abstract=2409811 [Retrieved October 15, 2020].)

In the study, the law professors reported the "results from a series of experiments in which subjects were presented with a pair of images and asked to assess the similarity between the two works using the criteria ordinarily given to fact-finders" (usually jurors) "for the substantial similarity determination."

When the subjects were given additional information about "the simple fact of copying" or the creative efforts expended on the protected work, the law professors saw a significant upwards variation in the subjects' assessments of similarity. This suggested that fact-finders in infringement cases are sensitive to additional information presented as evidence about two competing works and the creators of those works, contrary to the existing law of substantial similarity.

Essentially, Professors Balganesh, Manta, and Wilkinson-Ryan concluded that the availability of the additional information and its salient effect actively distorted the fact-finders' assessments of the two works' similarity. Thus, it called into question the objectivity of the substantial similarity element of infringement.

Is the study helpful to you as a writer in determining whether you have written something that bears substantial similarity to a work by another author? Probably not. At best, you know that, if you are sued for infringement and the case goes to trial, the outcome may be a crap shoot. The safest course to sail through the unpredictable sea of copyright law is one you have carefully plotted, using accurate charts and information to avoid pirates who wish to board your boat, kidnap you, and make you one of them.

10

Remedies for Infringement

Monetary Damages and Injunctive Relief

Two legal remedies are available to an aggrieved party for infringement. These are monetary damages and injunctive relief. These damages for infringement are set out in the Copyright Act of 1976, as amended by Congress, at 17 U.S.C. § 504.

There are three categories of monetary damages: (a) actual damages; (b) the pirate's (infringer's) profits; and (c) statutory damages.

Actual damages, sometimes called compensatory damages, are the financial losses suffered by the copyright owner from the infringement. These may be lost sales, lost profits, or lost revenue from licensing. Other financial losses may be shown, provided there is a sufficient nexus between the infringement and the injury suffered by the copyright owner. But all financial losses must be capable of measurement in actual dollars and cents. Estimated losses will not cut the mustard in court.

On paper, this looks straightforward, right? In the real world, though, the journey from complaint to jury verdict is often a long and winding legal road. The burden of proof is on the copyright owner to demonstrate that the infringement was responsible for a decline in sales and that the decline in sales occurred almost immediately, in a calculated amount, after the infringement. Although the copyright owner may testify as a lay witness and state his or her opinion about the cause and amount of the loss, it is infinitely better to have an expert testify and explain to the jury the measure of damages, in the expert's opinion, and the exact amount of damages, in the expert's opinion, that were sustained by the copyright owner.

Ultimately, however, the judge will instruct the jury on the measure of damages applicable to the case (unless the parties agree to a bench trial, in which the judge decides the case based upon the evidence presented).

The profits earned by the pirate/infringer, if any, are always fair game for the copyright owner in a trial. Common sense governs here — why should a thief be allowed to benefit from stealing? The statute only requires the copyright owner to present proof of the infringer's gross revenue. The infringer is required to prove his or her "deductible expenses and the elements of profit attributable to factors other than the copyrighted work." The infringer's profits may be shown through cross-examination of the infringer, but the safest route to recovering these damages is to use an expert witness.

Who might qualify as an expert witness? An economist, for sure, or perhaps an individual with extensive experience in the publishing industry. The expert's credentials must be bona fide, however, for two reasons. One is that the defendant infringer, may hire their own expert to testify, turning the trial into a "battle of the experts." The second and most important reason, though, is that the infringer's attorney may challenge the qualifications of the copyright owner's expert witness, resulting in a ruling by the U.S. District Court judge that the plaintiff copyright owner's expert is not competent to testify. Such an unfavorable ruling could blow your case out of the water.

(By the way, the legal mechanism for disqualifying a party's expert is utilized before a trial, and is accomplished by filing a motion. The standard used by the court in deciding the motion was laid down by SCOTUS in *Daubert v. Merrell Dow Pharmaceuticals, Inc.*, 509 U.S. 579 (1993). If you want to confound your fellow authors at a cocktail party, ask them if they know the correct pronunciation of "Daubert.")

The third category of damages, statutory damages, is found in the Copyright Act of 1976 and is specific as to the amounts. Proving statutory damages may be an easier task than proving lost sales and/or the infringer's profits, but registration of the copyright with the U.S. Copyright Office is a prerequisite to seeking statutory damages. There is a trap for the unwary here, though. The registration has to be done either within three months after the creation of the work or no later than one month after discovery of the infringement. Failure to comply with these registration deadlines precludes the recovery of statutory damages.

If the copyright owner has complied with the prerequisites of 17 U.S.C. § 504(c)(1) for seeking statutory damages, the copyright owner is entitled to recover for "any one work, for which any one infringer is liable individually, or for which two or more infringers are liable jointly and severally," a minimum damage award of $750 and a maximum damage award of $30,000. The court must consider the award as just, and if the work is a compilation or a derivative work, all parts are treated as one work for purposes of the damages award.

If the copyright owner can prove to the satisfaction of the court that the infringement was willful, the copyright owner can request the court to increase the statutory damages to a maximum of $150,000.

But if the infringer can prove to the court's satisfaction that the infringement was unintentional, the trial judge has the discretion to decrease the damage award to $200. The statute also provides protection to the infringer from a damage award based upon the infringer's reasonable belief that the infringement was a fair use, provided the infringer was affiliated with a nonprofit educational institution, a library, archives, or a public broadcasting entity and certain other conditions are shown by the infringer.

The copyright owner may show (and establish a "rebuttable presumption") that the infringement was willful by proof that the infringer acted alone or with another person to knowingly provide "materially false contact information" to the registrar of a domain name; a domain name registry; or other "domain name registration authority." Yet, 17 U.S.C. § 504 (c)(3)(C) is fuzzy on its application to copyright infringement by improper use of a domain name, because it refers to the "Trademark Act of 1946," found at 15 U.S.C. §1127 for the definition of a domain name. This subsection of the damages statute appears to apply to trademark infringements.

But 17 U.S.C. § 504(d), the last paragraph of the statute, reverts to the term "copyrighted work" by providing an additional penalty for the defendant infringer who did not have reasonable grounds to believe the use was exempt. The copyright owner can recover, additionally, double the amount of the license fee that the infringer should have paid the plaintiff copyright owner. The double damage award for failure to pay the license fee is limited to a maximum of three years, however.

If you are a copyright owner victimized by an infringement, the damages provided for in the Copyright Act of 1976 should give you comfort. But what if you are on the receiving end of a claim of infringement and receive a copyright infringement notice from the copyright owner's lawyer(s)? The answer to this question is simple. Get thee hence to a copyright lawyer for advice!

Injunctive relief is an equitable remedy. An equitable remedy is a remedy fashioned by courts when the law is inadequate to make an injured party whole. In other words, money damages alone are not enough to compensate the injured plaintiff for the wrong suffered at the hands of the defendant. Injunctive relief is considered an extraordinary remedy.

A U.S. District Court has the judicial power to grant an injunction to the copyright owner in an infringement case. An injunction is an order by the court prohibiting an act by the defendant infringer or commanding the defendant infringer to do something. A District Court may issue a preliminary (sometimes referred to as temporary) injunction and/or a permanent injunction.

A preliminary injunction is sought by the plaintiff copyright owner when the infringement lawsuit is filed. Usually, the preliminary injunction is used to halt the distribution and sales of the copyright owner's work by the infringer for a limited duration, pending determination of the ultimate issues in the lawsuit. The injunction stays in place for the length of time ordered by the court, until a full and complete hearing can be conducted.

A permanent injunction may be ordered by the court upon the entry of a final judgment in the case. The permanent injunction may command the infringer to forever stop distributing, selling, reproducing or creating works that are derivative of the copyright owner's original work.

An injunction, whether preliminary or permanent, is a powerful remedy. For this reason, the party seeking injunctive relief must prove two things. First, they must show that an immediate threat of irreparable harm exists. Second, they must show that there is no adequate remedy at law for the harm that is threatened.

My discussion of the controversy between the epic *Gone With the Wind* and the parody, *The Wind Done Gone*, is illustrative of injunctive relief for alleged infringement.

11

The United States Copyright Office

The Very Useful, Most Helpful Copyright Compendium

If you are contemplating filing your own copyright application, please think twice. Granted, you may not have the money to consult a copyright lawyer (they are expensive), but you should at least have a licensed attorney examine your copyright application before you submit it. The money you pay an attorney for advice and consultation may save you money in the future. Trial lawyer and U.S. President Abraham Lincoln reportedly said, "He who represents himself has a fool for a client."[1]

That said, if you insist on pursuing your own copyright application, you should obtain a copy of and consult the *Compendium of U.S. Copyright Office Practices* before doing anything. The *Compendium* is a manual compiled and produced by the United States Copyright Office, a branch of the Library of Congress, for

---

[1] Although this quote is almost always attributed to Lincoln, research indicates that the originator of the saying may be anonymous and is possibly an old Italian proverb.

use by the Copyright Office staff as a general guide to registration, deposit, and copyright recordation policies and procedures. Its third edition was released by the Copyright Office on August 19, 2014, with a revised version being published on September 29, 2017.

Unlike the 1976 Copyright Act, as amended, or the Copyright Office rules and regulations, the *Compendium* does not have the force of law. Courts have relied upon and cited it as persuasive authority, however, and because of the Copyright Office's specialized experience with copyright law, courts have accorded deference to the *Compendium* in resolving copyright disputes. Furthermore, it is the only written authority on certain issues, such as whether a government body may copyright laws it has enacted. Attorneys sometimes use the *Compendium* when dealing with the Copyright Office, but interestingly, this seems uncommon.

Nevertheless, I advocate consulting the *Compendium* in advance of any *pro se* (representation by oneself, instead of by a lawyer) efforts to gain approval of a copyright application from the U.S. Copyright Office. Consulting it can certainly do no harm; an error in registration or deposit of copyright can result in the rejection of your application.

12

Securing Copyright in the United States

Practicing Safe Copyright

The common belief that a copyright must be registered to protect it is a misconception. Copyright protection is automatic as soon as a work is created in a fixed, tangible form. There is no requirement of publication, no registration requirement, and no other requirement you must meet to secure your copyright. Publication of a work, however, is important to copyright owners because it puts other creators of works on notice of your copyright.

Publication is defined in the 1976 Copyright Act as the distribution of copies or "phonorecords" of a work.[1] The copies or phonorecords should display the copyright notice in a manner sufficient to give others reasonable notice of the claimed copyright. Although the notice can appear on the phonorecord label or

---

[1] The Copyright Act of 1909 required publication of a work. However, the Copyright Act of 1976 eliminated publication as a requirement for securing a copyright.

container, the better practice is to affix the notice on the copies or phonorecords. The Copyright Office has regulations governing the form of the copyright notice and its position. These may be found in the Code of Federal Regulations (37 C.F.R. Part 202.20). However, *Circular 3, Copyright Notice,* published by the Copyright Office, explains the requirements for form and notice.[2]

Registration by the copyright owner is voluntary. The advantage of registration, which may be done at any time during the life of a copyright, lies in bringing an action against an individual or entity alleging copyright infringement. Registration serves as evidence of the date of creation of the work by the copyright owner. Yet, if that date is disputed in an infringement action, the registration also serves as evidence of the existence of the copyright on the registration date.

Note that registration of a copyright is effective on the date the Copyright Office receives the submission of the application in proper form, with the required elements. The length of time the Copyright Office takes to process a registration application and issue a certificate of registration does not affect the effective date of the registration.

An application to register a copyright may be submitted by mail to the U.S. Copyright Office at the following address:

Library of Congress
Copyright Office-DOC, LM 433
101 Independence Avenue SE
Washington, DC 20559-6000

An application to register a copyright can also be submitted electronically through the registration portal. The Copyright Office prefers electronic registration for basic literary works; works

---

[2] https://www.copyright.gov/circs/circ03.pdf

of visual art; and performing arts works, including motion pictures, sound recordings, and single serial issues. Group registration of serial issues must be done electronically. Also, published and unpublished photographs, unpublished works, serials, newsletters, newspapers, applications to register an architectural work, and applications to amplify or supplement existing registrations must be completed and submitted online.

There are several advantages of electronic registration. The processing time for electronic registration is faster than registration by mail. Also, electronic registration provides status tracking of the registration application; online payment of fees; and the option to send a physical copy of a work or to upload certain categories of works. Visit the Copyright Office's website at www. copyright.gov to register a work electronically.

Following Instructions

You must follow the Copyright Office instructions to the letter for the submission of your application. The copyright application must be accompanied by a properly prepared Form DCS (Document Cover Sheet) in the same envelope or package and (1) the document to be recorded; (2) the proper filing fee; and (3) any additional material being provided in connection with your submission, such as an electronic title list, English translation of non-English material, written justification for certain redacted material, an additional copy of the completed FORM DCS to be file stamped by the Copyright Office, and a self-addressed postage-paid envelope for a return receipt.

Here is the hyperlink to Form DCS, along with the instructions for completing it:[3] https://www.copyright.gov/forms/for

---

[3] A link to this form, as well as other U.S. Copyright Office forms mentioned in this chapter, is being furnished in lieu of printing a reproduction of the forms. A reduction of the forms sufficient to fit on the pages of this book would be difficult

mdcs.pdf.

Here are the URLs for the U.S. Copyright Office's copyright application forms for each different fixed, tangible medium of expression:

https://www.copyright.gov/forms/formtx.pdf
https://www.copyright.gov/forms/formse.pdf
https://www.copyright.gov/forms/formpa.pdf
https://www.copyright.gov/forms/formsr.pdf

Application Fees

The registration fees charged by the U.S. Copyright Office are published in *Circular 4*. Here is the link to the fee page in *Circular 4*: https://www.copyright.gov/about/fees.html. The fee amounts are current as of March 20, 2020.

The filing fee for electronic registration is much less than registration using paper forms. The standard filing fee for electronic registration of basic claims is $65, but if you register only one work; it is not a work made for hire; and you are the only author and the only claimant, the filing fee is only $45.

The fee for basic registration using paper forms is $125, payable by check or money order. You cannot pay for basic registration by credit card unless you hand deliver the paper forms to the Copyright Office Public Information Office, located at:

U.S. Copyright Office
James Madison Memorial Building
101 Independence Avenue SE
Washington, DC 20559

Several other fees are charged by the Copyright Office for

to read without a magnifying glass.

myriad services. These include fees for searching copyright records and preparing an official report (which can be as high as $400, at a rate of $200 per hour, with a two hour minimum; fees for the retrieval and copying of records (usually a minimum of ($200); fees for recordation of documents; fees for removal of personally identifiable information; and miscellaneous fees, including service charges for delivery of documents via Federal Express or facsimile.

The different fees charged by the Copyright Office for different services are too numerous to list here and may change from time to time. Before applying for registration or requesting any other service from the Copyright Office, you should consult the most up-to-date version of *Circular 4.*

13

Securing International Copyright Protection

Is My U.S. Copyright Any Good across the Pond?

In 1973, the Doobie Brothers, a popular rock band, released a song titled "China Grove." Tom Johnston, a member of the band, composed the song after passing through the small town of China Grove, in Bexar County, Texas, on his way to a Doobie Brothers concert in San Antonio. But the Doobie Brothers' "China Grove" was fictional. Johnston sang in the recording about a town with a sizable Asian population and a wacky sheriff who behaved in an erratic manner, neither of which was true.

The song became a radio hit and put the China Grove in Bexar County on the United States and State of Texas maps. Yet, the real China Grove, Texas, named for a grove of chinaberry trees once located near the town's former train depot, did not have either a large number of Chinese residents or a crazy sheriff.

Meanwhile, the Doobie Brother's "China Grove," was recorded 32 years after author Eudora Welty's 1941 short story, "Why I Live at the P.O." In Ms. Welty's story, the female protagonist set up housekeeping at the post office in the fictional town of China Grove, Mississippi, to escape her eccentric family.

Finally, to further confuse music and literary aficionados, there is another, real China Grove in North Carolina.

But how does this story relate to the registration by a writer of a copyright in a foreign country?

I offer this brief frolic and detour as an allegory to illustrate the haphazard nature of international copyright protection. International law, contrary to what most U.S. citizens think, does not exist in the form of one code composed of statutes universally binding all world nations. International law is a patchwork quilt stitched together by various treaties and conventions signed or joined by some nations and ignored by others.

This holds true for international copyright law, even though there is a considerable body of international copyright law universally followed by many nations. There are China Groves everywhere, but not all of them follow identical copyright registration laws. Thus, securing international copyright protection poses a conundrum for the U.S. author who wants to sell a book across the pond.

In the interest of full disclosure, the complicated subject matter of international copyright law is beyond my ken and thus, it is beyond the scope of this book. If you become an international best-selling author, your literary agent and publishing house will undoubtedly take the lead on protecting your copyright in foreign countries. Be thankful for big favors.

You should not be surprised, then, to learn that some countries do not have a central copyright office or agency. In fact, some countries do not even have copyright laws, and the countries that do may not offer the same protection available to authors who create works in the United States. Copyright laws may vary from country to country. It is likely that the legal terminology used in one country will be different from that used in another country. Furthermore, if the same term is used in two or more countries' copyright laws, the term may have different meanings, possibly due to language differences.

Mark Twain, author of the best-selling travel book of all time, *The Innocents Abroad, or The New Pilgrims' Progress,* understood this. When Twain published this book (the best-selling of Twain's works during his lifetime) in 1869, he humorously chronicled his "Great Pleasure Excursion" on board the chartered vessel *Quaker City,* observing and critiquing the nuances between cultures and societies as he traveled through Europe and the Holy Land in 1867 with a group of Americans.

For Twain, nothing was sacred. Twain lampooned his fellow travelers, himself, travelogues by other authors, the natives of the countries and regions that he visited, and their languages and vocabularies. A consummate wordsmith also adept at sarcasm, Twain once remarked, "The difference between the almost right word and the right word is really a large matter — 'tis the difference between the lightning-bug and the lightning."

Twain's analogy might be a good thing to remember when undertaking (with expert assistance) the registration of your copyright in countries across the pond. If your work is also printed in a foreign language, caution is advised. The copyright to your work may require registration in each language.

The United States Copyright Office's *Circular 38A, International Copyright Relations of the United States,* offers a brief overview of international conventions, treaties and other bilateral agreements the U.S. has made with foreign countries affecting copyrights. *Circular 38A* also summarizes the participation of foreign countries in these treaties and conventions. The information in *Circular 38A* is current as of August 2020.

Importantly, there is no "international copyright" automatically protecting an author's writings worldwide. Protection against unauthorized use of a writer's work in a foreign country is dependent upon that country's national laws.

Thankfully, protection is available to American authors through the World Intellectual Property Organization (WIPO), which administers the Berne Convention for the Protection of Literary and Artistic Works. The WIPO also administers the WIPO Copyright Treaty; the WIPO Performances and Phonograms Treaty; the Geneva Convention for the Production of Phonograms Against Unauthorized Duplication of Their Phonograms; the Brussels Convention Relating to the Distribution of Program-Carrying Signals Transmitted by Satellite; and the Marrakesh Treaty to Facilitate Access to Published Works for Persons Who Are Blind, Visually Impaired, or Otherwise Print Disabled.

But I have not finished the list. More acronyms are on the way.

There is also the Universal Copyright Convention, administered by the United Nations Educational, Scientific and Cultural Organization (UNESCO). Moreover, the World Trade Organization (WTO) administers the Agreement or Trade-Related Aspects of Intellectual Property Rights (TRIPS). The latter is a multilateral trade agreement containing obligations related to intellectual property rights, including copyright and enforcement measures.

The obligations in these treaties and conventions are substantive And not mere procedural devices for securing a copyright. Many of them also reference "points of attachment," which are the factors that allow an author's work eligible for protection to enjoy it in countries that are members of the treaty. The country where a work is first published and the author's nationality are points of attachment.

The Copyright Act is not completely lacking in international copyright protection. Sections 101 and 104A specify the scope of copyright protection available for both published and unpublished foreign works created by authors in other countries.

But to obtain copyright protection in a foreign country for a work you created in the United States, you must determine the points of attachment under that country's copyright laws. The scope or breadth of copyright protection in that country will be set by that country's substantive copyright laws and practices that pertain to a U.S. creative work.

It is important for you to determine what a foreign country's points of attachment are before you publish your manuscript anywhere for the first time, because the protection offered by that foreign country's copyright law may hinge upon the date of first publication.

If all of this seems too complicated to absorb, well, it is for most writers. Even IP attorneys who practice copyright law globally have full plates when trying to keep separate in their minds the different copyright practices of foreign nations. If you decide to go global with your novel, screenplay, stage play, nonfiction book, or other writings, you absolutely must seek legal advice from a competent international copyright attorney. A general practice lawyer will not be equipped with the tools to protect your creation. You must consult a specialist in international copyright law. Ding ding ding! Do I have your attention? I hope so!

Below is a list of countries from *Circular 38A* with which the U.S. may have (or perhaps previously had) bilateral agreements for international copyright protection or agreements through treaties or conventions. Bear in mind, though, that the worldwide COVID-19 Pandemic could possibly have an unforeseen effect on applying for copyright protection in these countries.

The countries include: Afghanistan, Albania, Algeria, Andorra, Antigua and Barbuda, Argentina (but don't cry over it), Armenia, Australia, Austria, Azerbaijan, Bahamas, Bahrain, Bangladesh, Barbados, Belarus, Belgium, Belize, Benin, Bhutan, Bolivia, Bosnia and Herzegovina (does this remind you of a list of countries in an opening ceremony for the Summer Olympic Games?), Botswana, Brazil, Brunel Darussalam, Bulgaria, Burkina Faso, Burundi,

Cambodia, Cameroon, Canada, Cape Verde, Central African Republic, Chad, Chile, China, Colombia, Comoros, Democratic Republic of the Congo, Congo, Cook Islands, Costa Rica, Cote d'Ivoire, Croatia, Cuba, Cyprus, Czech Republic, Denmark, Djibouti, Dominica, Dominican Republic, Ecuador, Egypt, El Salvador, Equatorial Guinea, Estonia, Eswatini (formerly Swaziland), European Union, Fiji, Finland, France, Gabon, The Gambia, Georgia, Germany, Ghana, Greece, Grenada, Guatemala, Guinea, Guinea-Bissau, Guyana,

Haiti, Holy See, Honduras, Hong Kong, China, Hungary, Iceland, India, Indonesia, Ireland, Israel, Italy, Jamaica, Japan, Jordan, Kazakhstan, Kenya, Kiribati, Democratic People's Republic of North Korea, Republic of Korea, Kuwait, Kygyz Republic, Lao People's Democratic Republic, Latvia, Lebanon, Lesotho, Liberia, Libya, Liechtenstein, Lithuania, Luxembourg, Macau, China, Madagascar, Malawi, Malaysia, Maldives, Mali, Malta, Marshall Islands, Mauritania, Mauritius, Mexico, Federated States of Micronesia, Moldova, Monaco, Mongolia, Montenegro, Morocco, Mozambique, Union of Myanmar,

Namibia, Nauru, Nepal, Netherlands, New Zealand, Nicaragua, Niger, Nigeria, Niue, North Macedonia, Norway, Oman, Pakistan, Panama, Papua New Guinea, Paraguay, Peru, Philippines, Poland, Portugal, Qatar, Romania, Russian Federation (surprise!), Rwanda, Saint Kitts and Nevis, Saint Lucia, Saint Vincent and the Grenadines, Samoa, San Marino, Sao Tome and Principe, Saudi Arabia, Senegal, Serbia, Seychelles, Sierra Leone, Singapore, Slovakia, Slovenia, Solomon Islands, South Africa, Spain, Sri Lanka, Sudan, Suriname, Sweden, Switzerland, Syria, Taiwan (Chinese Taipei),

Tajikistan, Tanzania, Thailand, Togo, Tonga, Trinidad and

Tobago, Tunisia, Turkey, Turkmenistan, Tuvalu, Uganda, Ukraine, United Arab Emirates, United Kingdom, Uruguay, Uzbekistan, Vanuatu, Venezuela, Viet Nam, Yemen, Zambia, and Zimbabwe.

The following countries are not signatories to a treaty or convention to which the United States is a party: Eritrea, Ethiopia, Iran, Iraq.

Somewhat puzzling and unclear is the status of the following countries regarding international copyright relations with the United States, according to the Copyright Office: Palau, Somalia, Republic of South Sudan, Timor Leste. The U.S. Copyright Office designates the status of these countries as unclear because they may not have established copyright relations with the United States but may be honoring obligations incurred under a former political status, including possible relationships as a territory.

(Note: It is unclear to me why the Copyright Office is unable to arrive at an affirmative or negative status for these countries. It seems to me the United States of America should be able to determine whether it has a copyright law relationship with these countries.)

A major concern in registration of a copyright in a foreign country is whether your lawyer is licensed to practice copyright law in that country. The requirements for eligibility to perform particular legal tasks may (and often do) vary from one jurisdiction to another. If you publish a book that sells so well in America that your publisher advocates international sales, you should consult your literary agent to make sure the publisher uses a copyright lawyer in each jurisdiction who is admitted to practice before that jurisdiction's copyright office or agency. If that lawyer is not properly admitted to practice copyright law in that jurisdiction, someone might challenge your copyright as invalid on the grounds it was illegally submitted.

Yikes! This is a disaster which can be easily avoided; the sins of an errant IP lawyer should not be visited upon their writer client.

14

Copyright Law in the Digital Age

Lost in Cyberspace

The amorphous Internet — upon which surfs social media communication platforms such as YouTube, Twitter, Facebook, My Space, Instagram, LinkedIn (for business), Snapchat, Imgur, Flickr, Tumblr, Tik Tok, WhatsApp, Caffeine and many others, and through which search engines such as Google and Yahoo, Bing, Duck Duck Go, and Ask.com are available — has raised questions never before encountered about the protection of intellectual property rights. The purpose of copyright law is to protect original material upon its creation. The creator holds the exclusive rights to reproduce their work, distribute it, and create additional works derived from their original creation ("derivative" works). But digital transmission of creative works via the Internet has revolutionized the idea of what constitutes illegal copying of a protected work.

Does uploading a copyrighted document or a media file; retransmitting a posting on social media without permission; or browsing material on the Internet through a laptop, tablet, or smart phone violate copyright and digital theft laws? It could.

On the other hand, digital use of copyrighted materials in one of these ways arguably might be the same as reading a book in a library or browsing through a magazine at a newsstand — only digitally. If reading copyrighted materials in a library or at a newsstand does not constitute copyright infringement, why should an individual who reads these works digitally be treated differently? Could that possibly be a violation of the Constitution's Equal Protection clause?

These copyright issues did not arise overnight, but it appears they will not be resolved in the near future.

As early as 1997, the Washington Post and five other news organizations sued several Internet news websites for copyright infringement. The gravamen of the complaint was that the Internet news websites were repackaging and republishing for profit media worldwide web pages. The WaPo and co-plaintiffs alleged the news sites were using protected trademarks for links and were running ads with the republished copyrighted material that lined the pockets of the pirates, instead of the copyright holders.

Alas, the case was settled out of court (as it should have been), so there was no judicial precedent established that answered the questions raised by the lawsuit.

But the Digital Age has produced other copyright controversies. The bedrock of copyright law is that a creative work must be original, and it must be fixed in a tangible medium. Is material created electronically on a PC or Mac and transmitted electronically "fixed in a tangible medium?" Is "cyberspace" akin to the airwaves? A live broadcast is not copyrightable because it is not fixed in a tangible medium. But if a live broadcast is simultaneously preserved on videotape, in an audio recording, or in digital files, does that constitute being "fixed in a tangible medium?" It does.

No one would argue (except the most obstinate person) that saving a document on a hard drive, CD, or DVD does not constitute fixing the original in "tangible medium." Copyrighted CDs and DVDs are sold commercially 24/7 through Amazon and other shopping websites. Yet, is intellectual property created but not saved on a laptop or tablet computer, then transmitted over the Internet, "fixed in a tangible medium?"

The "Sony Bono Digital Millennium Copyright Term Extension Act of 1998" which extended protection to copyright owners which would have expired under the Copyright Act of 1976 was upheld by a 7-2 vote of the Supreme Court on January 15, 2003 in *Eldred v. Ashcroft,* 537 U.S. 186 (2003). The Act arguably placed copyright law and the First Amendment at odds.

The plaintiffs in *Eldred,* anticipating the entry of many copyrighted works into the public domain, lost an opportunity for creative expression protected by the First Amendment. Justices Stevens and Breyer dissented because they felt the Act stifled the "creation and dissemination of information." Mickey Mouse (as I previously mentioned) gained another 20 years of copyright protection and so did many other iconic 20th Century entertainment figures.

Music Piracy

The lion's share of litigation over Internet piracy in the Digital Millennium has been concerned with copyright infringement of sound (music) recordings and movies. Current law in this area protects Internet Service Providers (ISP) from liability for the illegal distribution of pirated copies through the Internet, treating them like traditional telephone and telegraph companies. The latter were afforded liability at common law (legal precedent established by courts when deciding cases) by a qualified privilege (a protection from liability for acting in good faith or on trust in justifiable reliance on an act of another determined to be wrongful).

If you are a music aficionado, you may know about the Napster.com litigation in 2000 when that music website was sued by the rock band Metallica for copyright infringement and racketeering based upon Napster's distribution via free software allowing its users to swap copies of music in an MP3 digital format without a license. The litigation resulted in halting music bootlegging on the Internet and the demise of Napster.

Livestreaming

To qualify for a copyright, a work must be an original work fixed in a tangible medium of expression.

But does livestreaming (an online broadcast) an event constitute a "work?" This is a perplexing question. If the online broadcast is a livestream of a concert, art exhibition or a scholarly lecture, I suppose a credible argument could be made that it is a work. But what if the livestream is of a political campaign rally, a church service or a tour of a college campus? It seems doubtful either of these would qualify.

Yet, churches, in particular, have run into licensing issues over the use of copyrighted music during livestreamed worship services. There is no doubt that the music being performed is a work fixed in a tangible medium of expression. Fortunately, the religious service exemption in American copyright law allows the performance of copyrighted musical works during religious services without a license.

However, the religious service exemption does not apply to the broadcast of a religious service via online streaming. Therefore, a United Methodist Church congregation, for example, that livestreams a worship service during which copyrighted music is used must obtain a separate streaming license. But that license is only for congregational singing; it does not cover choir anthems.

Assuming *arguendo* that a livestreamed event is an original work, a second problem (besides whether "livestreamed" should be hyphenated or written as one word) must be solved. Is a livestreamed online broadcast fixed in a tangible medium of expression when it is merely a transitory event on the Internet?

If the online broadcast is simultaneously recorded, it seems a salient argument could be made that it is fixed in a tangible medium of expression. Professional sports broadcasts on television are zealously copyrighted by the networks. What is troubling, though, is the question of who is entitled to copyright a recorded livestream broadcast.

Does the copyright belong to the livestream broadcaster when the livestream is preserved as a recording? What if it is not recorded by the broadcaster but instead is "saved" by a person watching the livestream broadcast? If that person claims the livestream copyright, is their copyright superior to a subsequent claim of copyright by the broadcaster based upon the fact that the recording viewer had nothing to do with the broadcast? The latter seems logical, but if logic is to prevail, it must be legislated or judicially confirmed. The Digital Age is young, though. The legislative and judicial branches have all the time in the world to muck things up, yes?

Copyleft

This book is chiefly meant as a resource for the authors of traditional, printed written works. However, a brief word for writers who create nontraditional works is in order.

There is a practice now extent known as "copyleft." It should not be confused with the term "copyright," but it is a branch of copyright law.

"Copyleft" is a practice in which someone is granted the right to freely distribute and freely modify intellectual property, as long as the same intellectual property rights are preserved in works derived from the original. Copyleft uses licenses to preserve copyrights to computer software, documents, art, scientific discoveries, and even selected patents.

Copyleft software licenses are distinguishable from permissive free software licenses, however. A copyleft software license specifies that any information necessary to the modification and reproduction of the original must also be made available to any recipients of the software program. Usually, this information consists of source code files. These files contain a copy of the license terms and also acknowledge the source code's authors.

Examples of copyleft software are Mozilla Firefox, Java, and Open Office.

Copyright Law in the Future

Writers, and to a certain extent, photographers unfortunately are still pioneers on the digital frontier regarding judicial and statutory protection of their works transformed electronically and distributed via Internet piracy. When the founders of our country enshrined intellectual property in the Constitution's Copyright Clause, forward thinkers that they were, they surely did not contemplate a future of computers, cell phones, facsimile machines, and other electronic devices capable of sending emails, text messages and intellectual property from one American to another, or from, say, a Texas cowboy to a gaucho in Argentina or Uruguay. For that matter, they could not possibly have envisioned the development by scientific technology of artificial intelligence (AI).

United States and perhaps international copyright law seems ripe for an overhaul. We now are more than 20 years past the passage by Congress of the Digital Millennium Copyright Act of 1998. You as a writer may be able to take many necessary steps by contract to protect the originality of your manuscript, but if your book is scanned and uploaded by a pirate in Somalia who peddles it for profit to a bookseller in Eritrea, who do you sue and where do you sue them for infringement of the novel you penned and published in the United States of America?

What if several scenes of the play you wrote in Atlanta, Georgia are attached to an email without your permission and forwarded to a recipient in Los Angeles, California, but the email is routed through Nigeria, courtesy of an email server in Serbia, before it arrives in the LA resident's email inbox? Do you pursue relief solely under U.S. copyright law? What if the email server in Serbia is not shielded from liability under Serbian law, but it is under Nigerian law? Do you have to sue in multiple countries for injunctive relief to completely halt the distribution of your pirated play scenes?

What if, in the near future, AI becomes so sophisticated that a robot is capable of writing poetry? Is the poetry entitled to copyright protection? If so, to whom does the copyright belong? The creator of the robot? The designer of the robot's software? Or the robot, itself?

By now, you may be cursing me (justifiably so) for raising more questions than I have answered in this chapter. In all candor, however, I do not know the answers to these questions and, until writers are granted more specific copyright protection in the Digital Age and beyond, there may be a serious risk of plagiarism without a solid legal remedy. Pegleg pirates with hooks for hands may drop anchor, board your ship, plunder your intellectual property, and force you to walk the plank in your socks. Let's hope that does not happen, though. Let's hope that as the clock ticks toward the publication of your next brilliant creative story, copyright law opens wide its jaw and dispatches the pirates in a couple of bites.

Glossary of Copyright Law Terms

A

actual damages — monetary compensation for financial losses that can be proven to have occurred and for which the injured party has a legal right to be compensated.

B

burden of proof — standard that a party seeking to prove a legal claim in a civil action must satisfy by the introduction of legally competent, sufficient evidence.

C

Certiorari — an order issued by an appellate court agreeing to judicially reviews a decision of a lower court.

case citation — the official reference to a published decision of an appellate court.

code — a compilation of statutes enacted by Congress or the legislatures of individual states.

common law — law that is derived from custom and judicial precedent rather than by a statute.

compensatory damages — monetary compensation awarded by either a judge or jury in a civil case to compensate an injured party for loss or injury suffered as the result of an illegal act.

constitution — a document stating the fundamental principles by which the federal or a state government is authorized to govern its citizens.

copyright — the exclusive legal right to reproduce, copy, publish, sell, distribute or create a derivative of a literary, musical or artistic work fixed in a tangible medium of expression.

Copyright Act of 1976 — an act of Congress made effective in 1976 setting out United States copyright laws, including the Fair Use Doctrine, subsequently amended by Congress with additional copyright provisions.

Copyright Clause — Found in Article I, Section 8, Clause 8 of the United States Constitution, this clause confers upon the United States Congress the power "To promote the Progress of Science and useful Arts, by securing for limited Times to Authors and Inventors the exclusive Right to their respective Writings and Discoveries." It is the basis for intellectual property laws in the U.S., including copyright, patent and trademark laws.

D

defendant — the party who is sued in a civil case.

derivative work — a derivative work is the creation of a new work subsequent to an original, copyrighted work which includes major copyrightable elements of the original, first work.

E

enjoin — the issuance of an order by a court commanding a party to perform or refrain from performing a particular act.

equitable remedy — a judicial remedy fashioned by a court, based upon fairness, awarding legal relief to a party not specifically provided for in a statute.

F

Fair Use Doctrine — a doctrine in United States copyright law, codified by Congress in the U.S. Copyright Act of 1976, permitting the limited use of copyrighted material without having to first acquire permission from the copyright holder.

first sale — a legal doctrine which entitles a copyright owner to collect royalty payments the first time each copy of the copyright owner's work is sold. The purchaser of the work is permitted to resell or offer for rent their copy of the work without first obtaining permission from the copyright owner. However, the purchaser may not create a derivative work, reproduce the original work or publicly perform the work without permission.

H

holding — the legal principle forming the basis for an appellate court's opinion.

I

infringement — the exploitation, regardless of financial gain, of an exclusive, copyrighted work without the owner's permission.

injunction — a court order restraining an activity or commanding an affirmative act to undo a wrong.

intellectual property — a creative work or invention for which the creator has exclusive rights. either under a copyright, patent or trademark. In copyright law, it is generally a literary, artistic, or musical work.

Internet — often referred to as the "World Wide Web," it is an international network linking satellites and high speed broadband connections via computers for the purpose of distributing information.

J

jurisdiction — the legal subject matter over which a court may exercise its decision-making power. It is also the geographical area over which a court has the power to act. Furthermore, it is the power of a court over an individual or corporation which is a party to a lawsuit before the court.

L

licensing — the granting of express permission by a copyright owner, usually in exchange for monetary compensation, to publish or reproduce the copyright owner's work.

literary work — a creative written work of an author.

O

ownership — the exclusive right to sell, publish, distribute, license or reproduce a work held by its creator; the creator's employer; or by the purchaser of a copyright.

P

permanent injunction — a court order permanently restraining a particular act, such as the unauthorized distribution of a copyrighted work.

piracy — the theft of intellectual property and its resale for profit; sometimes referred to as bootlegging.

plaintiff — the party who files a civil lawsuit against another party or parties.

preliminary injunction — a court order temporarily halting an act alleged to be illegal by the plaintiff when filing a lawsuit.

prior restraint — the prohibition of publication of a work in violation of the First Amendment to the United States Constitution.

public domain — intellectual property no longer subject to copyright protection and available to use or exploit by anyone without permission.

R

registration — the obtaining by application and fees of a formal declaration of ownership of a copyright from the United States Copyright Office.

S

statute of limitations — the time period in which a civil action or criminal charge must be initiated. If initiated after the statute of limitations has "run," the right to pursue the civil or criminal action is forever lost.

statutory damages — damages specifically authorized by act of Congress codified in a statute.

summary judgment — a court ruling that no genuine issue of material fact exists in a civil lawsuit and thus one of the parties is entitled to a judgment as a matter of law, without a trial.

T

transformative — a legal concept by which a U.S. District Court determines whether the secondary use of a copyrighted work is a fair use or a copyright infringement. One factor in the determination is whether the secondary use added value to the original, copyrighted work.

W

work made for hire — a work prepared by an employee within the scope of his or her employment; the copyright is owned by the employer. A work for hire may also be created by contract between the creator and the commissioner of the work.

Made in the USA
Columbia, SC
16 December 2020